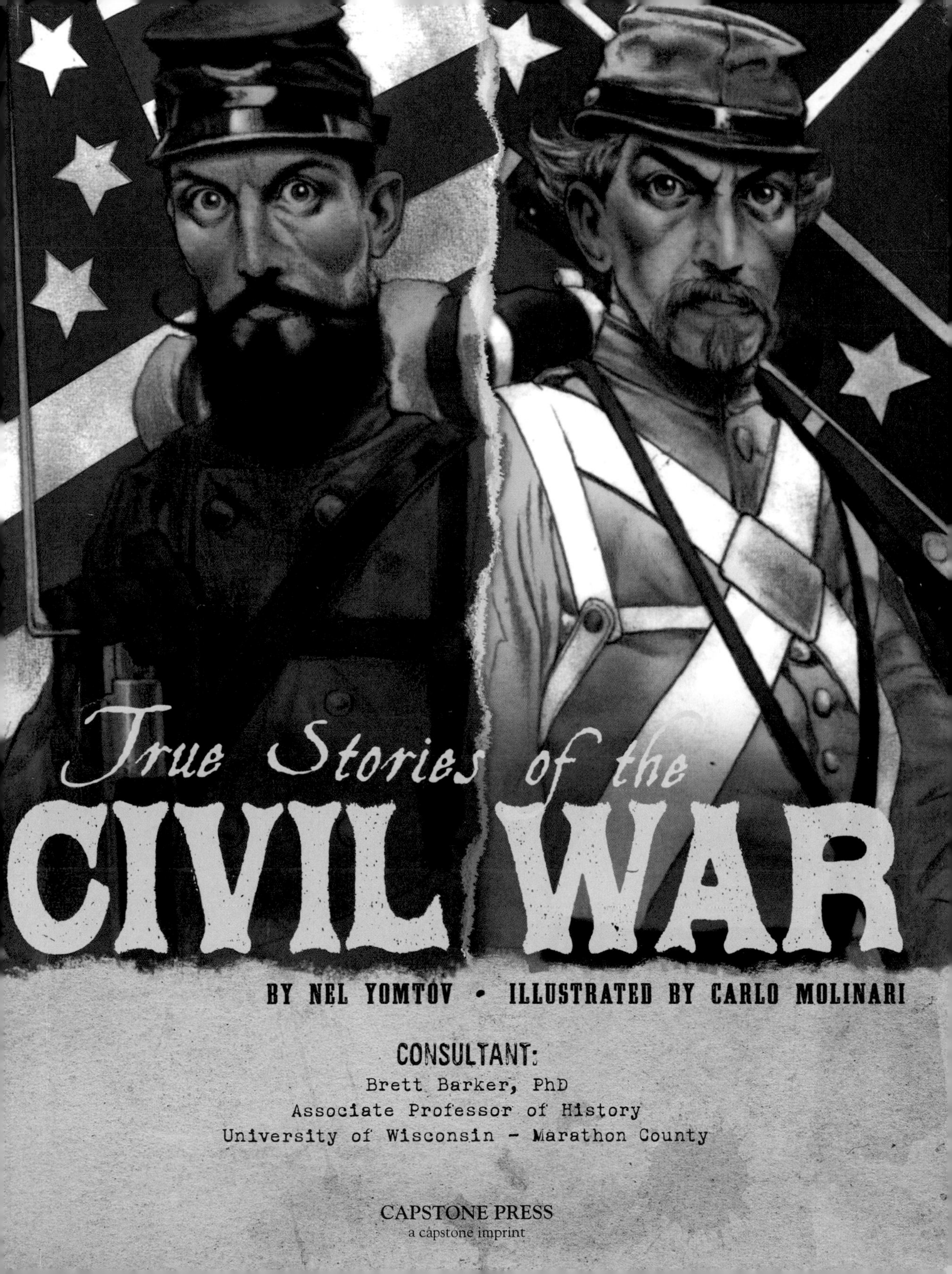

True Stories of the CIVIL WAR

BY NEL YOMTOV • ILLUSTRATED BY CARLO MOLINARI

CONSULTANT:
Brett Barker, PhD
Associate Professor of History
University of Wisconsin - Marathon County

CAPSTONE PRESS
a capstone imprint

Graphic Library is published by Capstone Press,
1710 Roe Crest Drive,
North Mankato, Minnesota 56003
www.capstonepub.com

Library of Congress Cataloging-in-Publication Data
Yomtov, Nelson.
True stories of the Civil War / by Nel Yomtov ; illustrated by Carlo Molinari.
pages cm. — (Graphic library. Stories of war)
Includes index.
Summary: "In graphic novel format, tells the stories of six men who fought for their beliefs during the Civil War"—Provided by publisher.
ISBN 978-1-4296-8624-2 (library binding)
ISBN 978-1-4296-9340-0 (paperback)
ISBN 978-1-62065-268-8 (ebook PDF)
1. United States—History—Civil War, 1861-1865—Biography—Comic books, strips, etc. 2. United States—History—Civil War, 1861-1865—Biography—Juvenile literature. 3. Graphic novels. I. Molinari, Carlo, illustrator. II. Title.
E467.Y66 2013
973.7—dc23 2012004276

Cover illustrated by Paul Davidson.

EDITOR: Jill Kalz

DESIGNER: Ashlee Suker

ART DIRECTOR: Nathan Gassman

PRODUCTION SPECIALIST: Laura Manthe

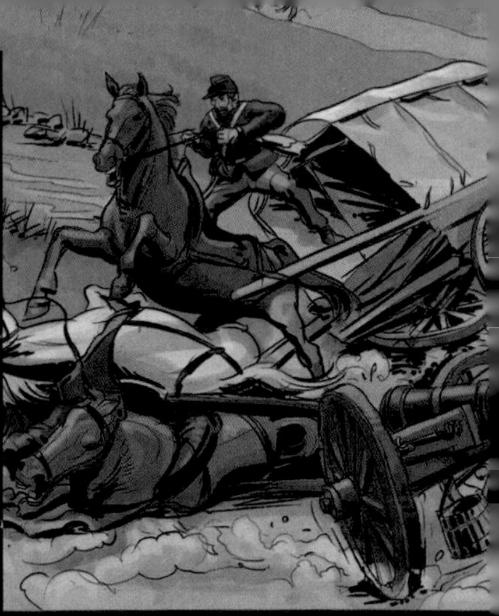

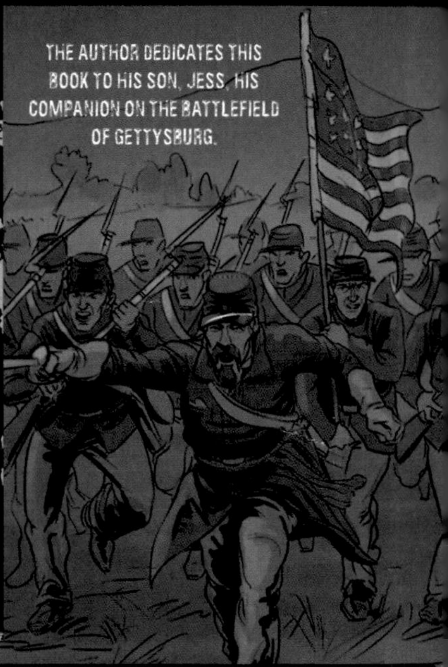
THE AUTHOR DEDICATES THIS BOOK TO HIS SON, JESS, HIS COMPANION ON THE BATTLEFIELD OF GETTYSBURG.

Editor's note: Direct quotations from primary sources are indicated by green text.

Direct quotations appear on the following pages:
Pages 6, 7, 8, 9 from "The First Shot of the Civil War: The Surrender of Fort Sumter, 1861," EyeWitness to History, www.eyewitnesstohistory.com <http://www.eyewitnesstohistory.com> (2006).
Pages 10, 11, 12, 13 from "The First Battle of Bull Run, 1861," EyeWitness to History, www.eyewitnesstohistory.com <http://www.eyewitnesstohistory.com> (2004).
Pages 14, 15, 16, 17, 18, 19 from "The Battle of the Ironclads, 1862," EyeWitness to History, www.eyewitnesstohistory.com <http://www.eyewitnesstohistory.com> (2005).
Pages 20, 21, 22, 23 from "Carnage At Antietam, 1862," EyeWitness to History, www.eyewitnesstohistory.com <http://www.eyewitnesstohistory.com> (1997).
Pages 25, 26, 27 from "Pickett's Charge, 1863," EyeWitness to History, www.eyewitnesstohistory.com <http://www.eyewitnesstohistory.com> (2010).
Pages 28, 29 from "The Last Stand by Lee's Army," by General John B. Gordon, http://www.historycentral.com/CivilWar/Surrender/Surrendergoron.html

Photo credits: illustration background by Jon Proctor, 2, 4, 30-31

Printed in the United States of America in Stevens Point, Wisconsin.
032012 006678WZF12

TABLE OF CONTENTS

CHAPTER 1
The U.S. Civil War: A Nation Torn 4

CHAPTER 2
Stephen Lee: The Attack on Fort Sumter 6

CHAPTER 3
Samuel English:
The Battle of the First Bull Run 10

CHAPTER 4
Samuel Dana Greene: Battle of the Ironclads . . . 14

CHAPTER 5
David Thompson: The Battle of Antietam 20

CHAPTER 6
General James Longstreet:
The Battle of Gettysburg 24

CHAPTER 7
General John Gordon: Surrender at Appomattox. . . 28

Glossary. 30
Read More 31
Internet Sites 31
Index 32

THE U.S. CIVIL WAR: A NATION TORN

The U.S. Civil War (1861–1865) was by far the deadliest conflict in U.S. history. And it nearly destroyed the young nation.

The road to war was paved with many disagreements between the Northern and Southern states. One of the biggest disagreements was over slavery. The South's economy depended on farming and slave labor. In the North, however, slavery was illegal. Many Northerners did not want new states joining the Union to be allowed to have slaves. Southerners worried that if the federal government became too strong, it would outlaw slavery everywhere. They feared that their way of life would be shattered. As the years passed, anger grew.

The South reached its breaking point when Abraham Lincoln was elected president in November 1860. Because of his strong support in the North, Southerners feared Lincoln would end slavery. Within weeks South Carolina withdrew, or seceded, from the Union. More Southern states soon followed. In February 1861 these states formed a new and independent government called the Confederate States of America (CSA), or the Confederacy.

On April 12, 1861, Confederate forces struck. They shelled the Union's Fort Sumter in South Carolina. Two days later Union forces inside the fort were forced to surrender. The Civil War had begun.

After four long years, the Union won the war. More than 620,000 Americans died from fighting and disease. Roughly 400,000 were wounded. Join six brave soldiers as they take you through the darkest, bloodiest war in U.S. history.

KEY DATES OF THE CIVIL WAR

APRIL 12, 1861: The war begins when Confederate forces attack the Union's Fort Sumter in South Carolina.

JULY 21, 1861: Confederate troops win the First Battle of Bull Run in Manassas, Virginia.

MARCH 9, 1862: The battle between the Union *Monitor* and the Confederate *Merrimac* ends in a draw.

APRIL 6–7, 1862: Union troops win the Battle of Shiloh in Tennessee.

SEPTEMBER 17, 1862: Union troops win the Battle of Antietam in Sharpsburg, Maryland.

MAY 1–4, 1863: Confederate forces claim victory at the Battle of Chancellorsville in Virginia.

JULY 1–3, 1863: Union troops win the Battle of Gettysburg in Pennsylvania.

MAY 5–7, 1864: The Battle of the Wilderness in Virginia ends in a draw.

APRIL 9, 1865: General Lee surrenders to the Union army, ending the Civil War.

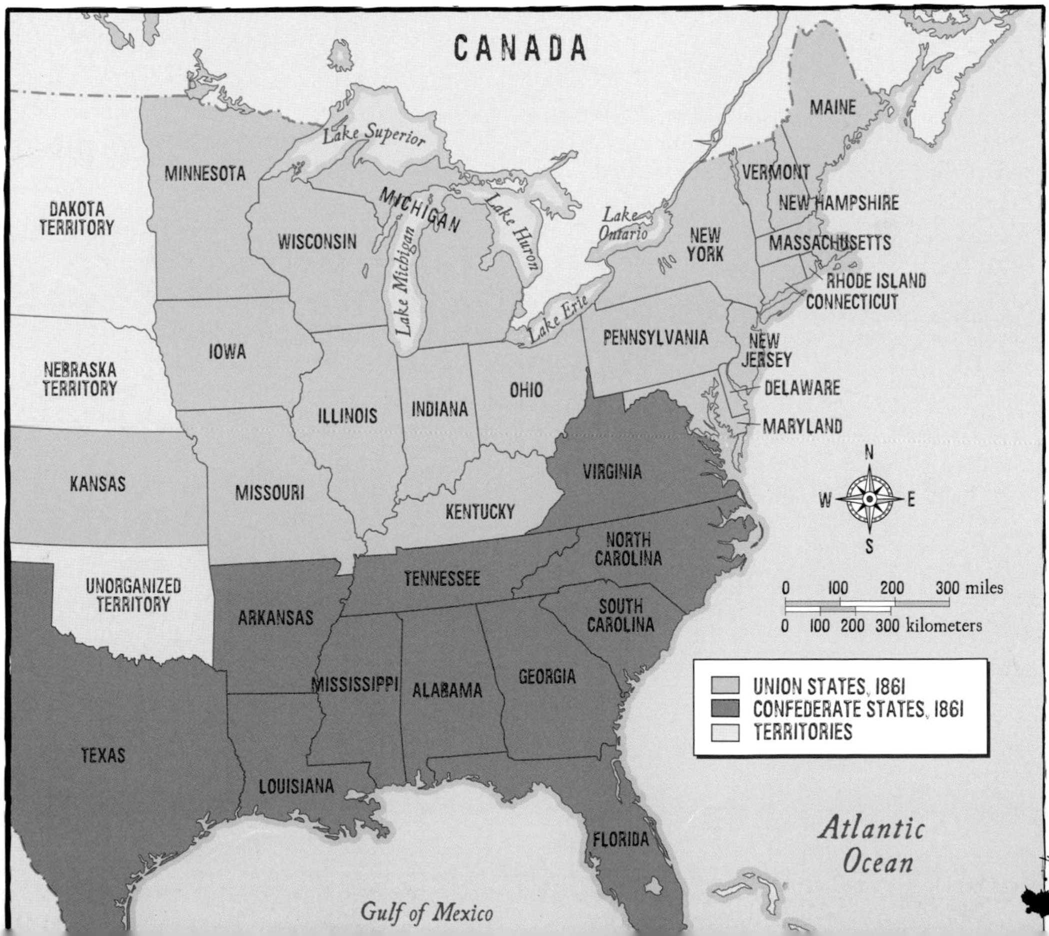
CANADA
Lake Superior
MAINE
MINNESOTA
VERMONT
NEW HAMPSHIRE
DAKOTA TERRITORY
MICHIGAN
Lake Huron
Lake Ontario
WISCONSIN
Lake Michigan
NEW YORK
MASSACHUSETTS
RHODE ISLAND
CONNECTICUT
Lake Erie
PENNSYLVANIA
IOWA
NEW JERSEY
NEBRASKA TERRITORY
DELAWARE
ILLINOIS
INDIANA
OHIO
MARYLAND
N
VIRGINIA
KANSAS
MISSOURI
W
E
KENTUCKY
S
NORTH CAROLINA
TENNESSEE
UNORGANIZED TERRITORY
0 100 200 300 miles
ARKANSAS
SOUTH CAROLINA
0 100 200 300 kilometers
GEORGIA
MISSISSIPPI
ALABAMA
UNION STATES, 1861
CONFEDERATE STATES, 1861
TERRITORIES
TEXAS
LOUISIANA
FLORIDA
Atlantic Ocean
Gulf of Mexico

CH. 2

Stephen Lee: The Attack on Fort Sumter

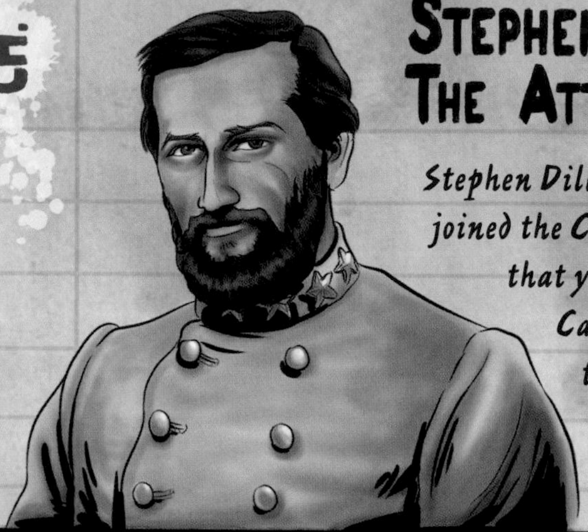

Stephen Dill Lee quit the U.S. Army in 1861 and joined the Confederate army as a captain. In April of that year, he was stationed at Charleston, South Carolina. He was put in command of one of the artillery companies that shelled Fort Sumter. Lee witnessed the first battle of the Civil War.

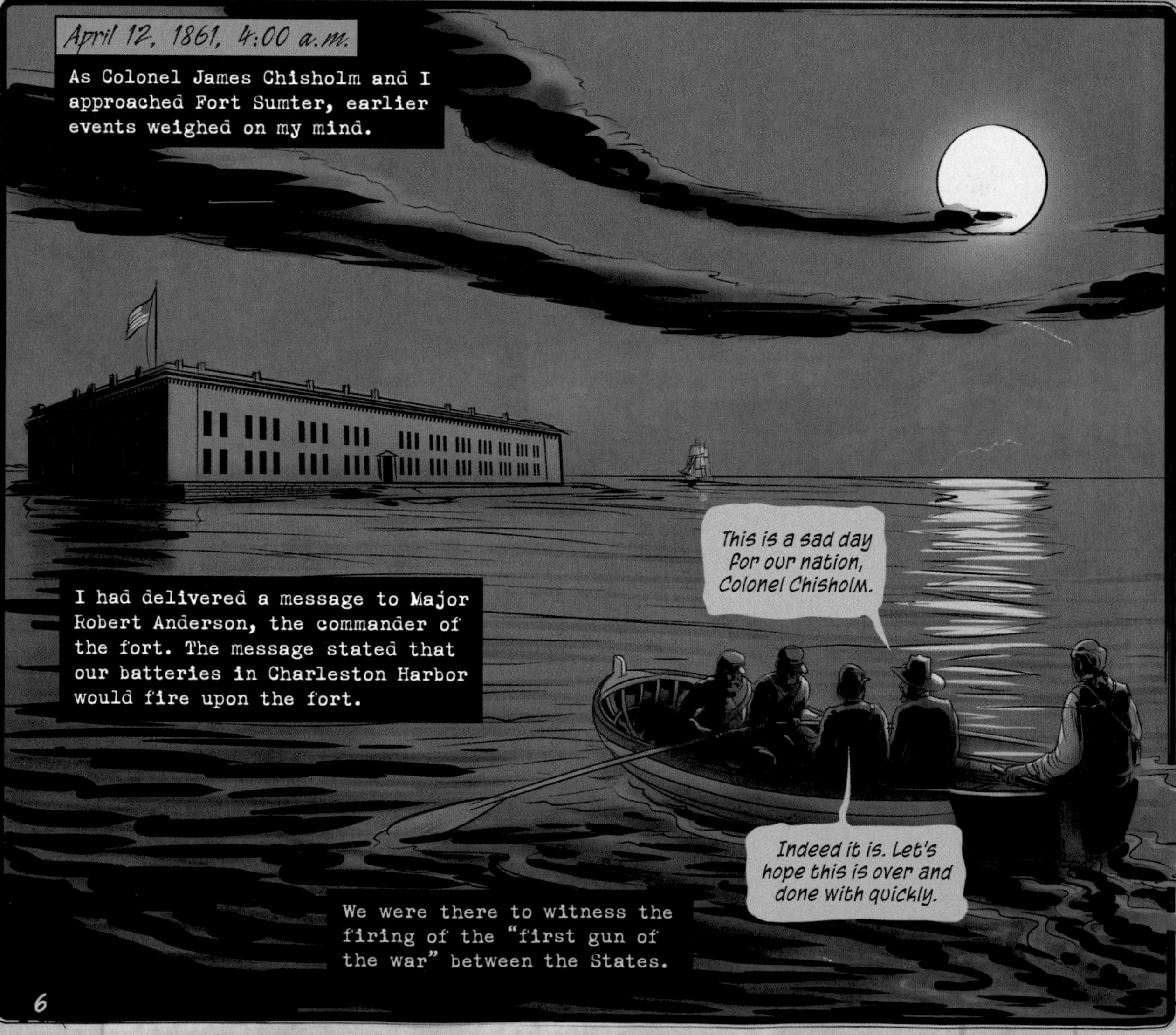
April 12, 1861, 4:00 a.m.
As Colonel James Chisholm and I approached Fort Sumter, earlier events weighed on my mind.
I had delivered a message to Major Robert Anderson, the commander of the fort. The message stated that our batteries in Charleston Harbor would fire upon the fort.
This is a sad day for our nation, Colonel Chisholm.
Indeed it is. Let's hope this is over and done with quickly.
We were there to witness the firing of the "first gun of the war" between the States.

The firing of the shell was a success. It burst immediately over the fort, apparently 100 feet above.

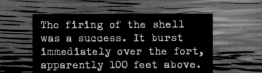

The firing of the mortar brought every soldier in the harbor to his feet, and every man, woman, and child in the city of Charleston from their beds.

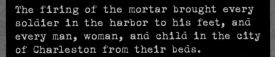

Look, Pa!

Fetch your mother and sisters. I want them to see this!

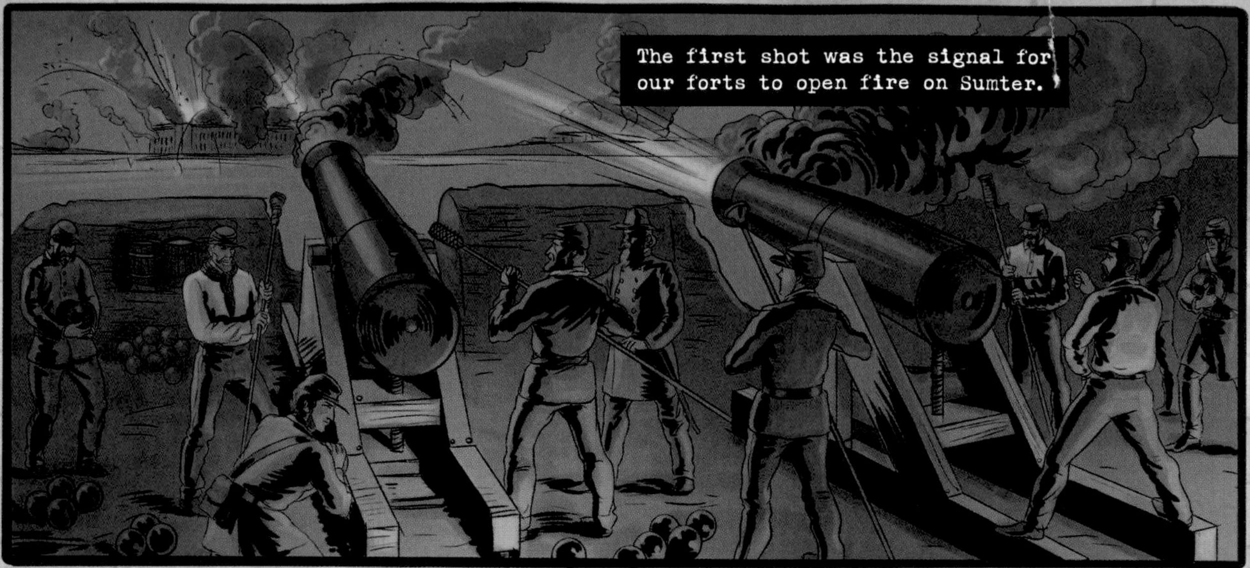
The first shot was the signal for our forts to open fire on Sumter.

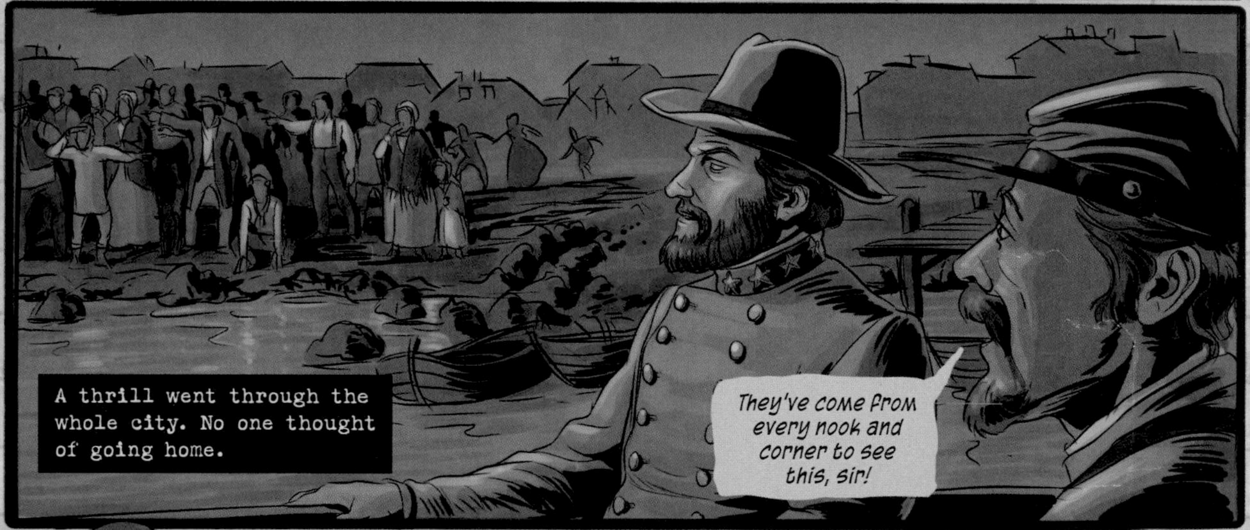
A thrill went through the whole city. No one thought of going home.
They've come from every nook and corner to see this, sir!

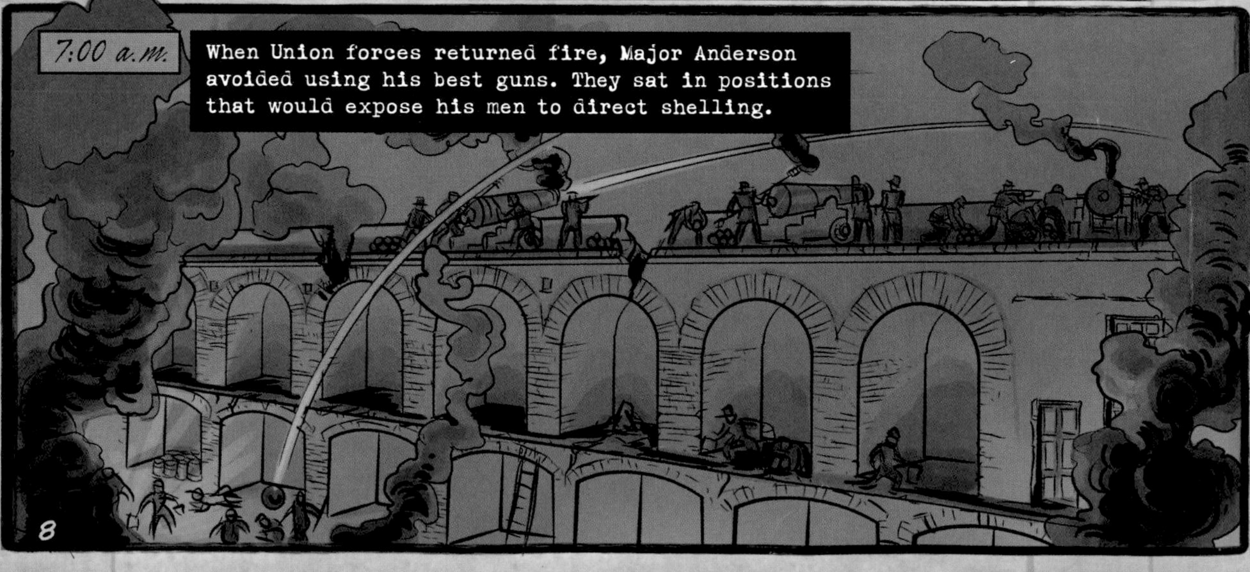
7:00 a.m.
When Union forces returned fire, Major Anderson avoided using his best guns. They sat in positions that would expose his men to direct shelling.

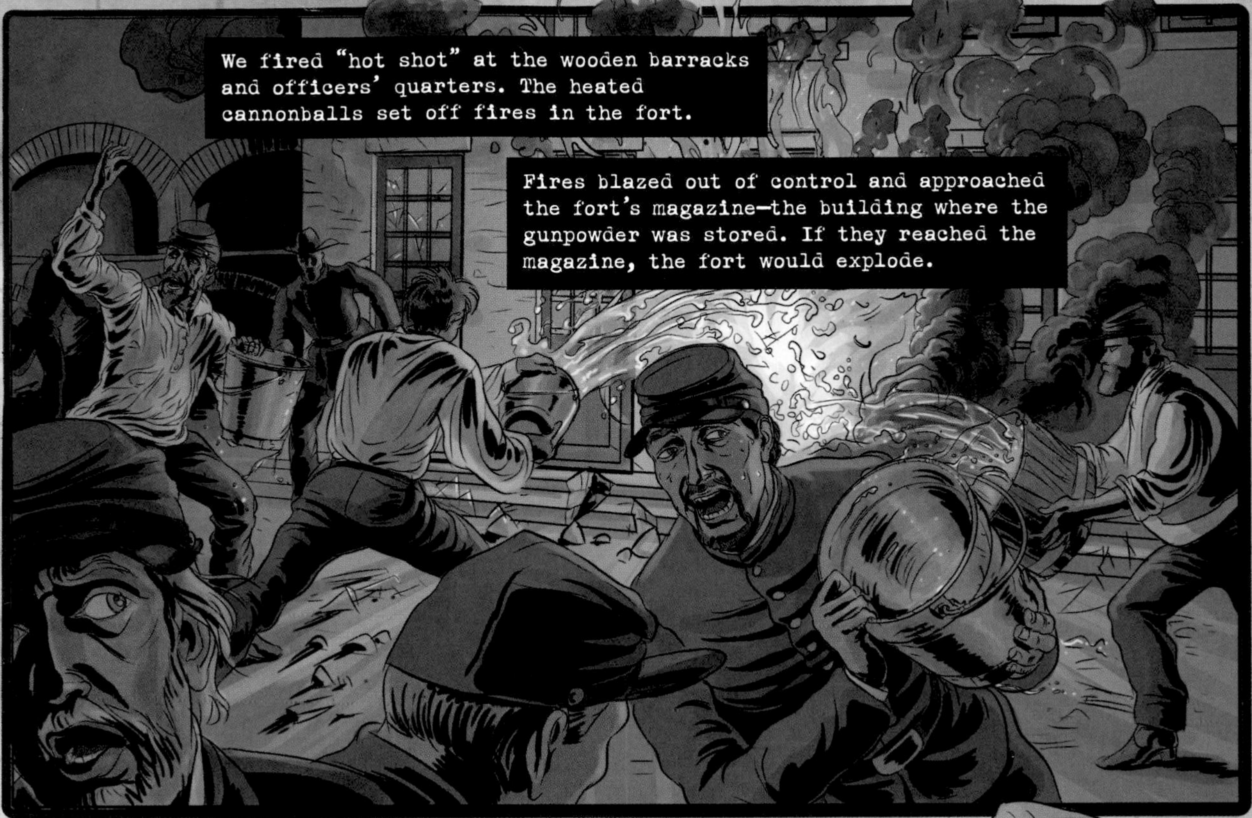
We fired "hot shot" at the wooden barracks and officers' quarters. The heated cannonballs set off fires in the fort.
Fires blazed out of control and approached the fort's magazine—the building where the gunpowder was stored. If they reached the magazine, the fort would explode.

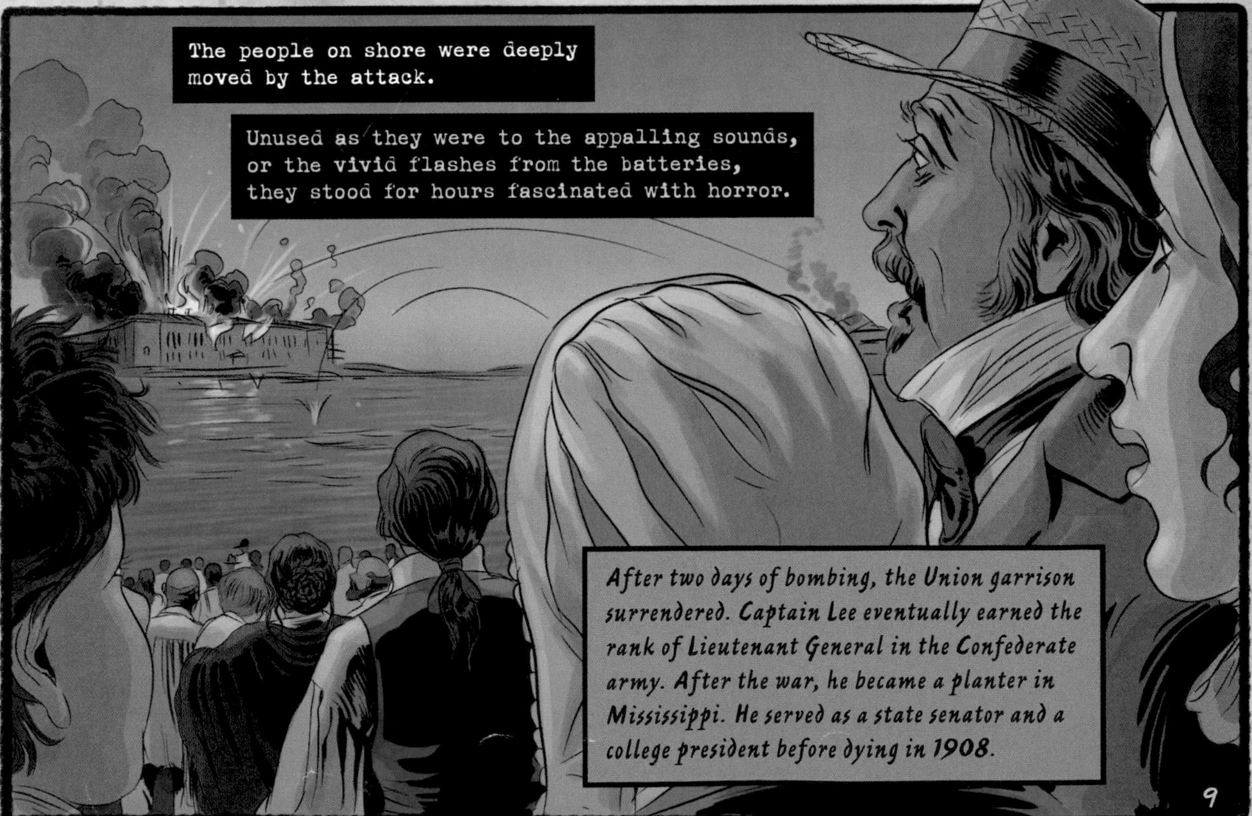
The people on shore were deeply moved by the attack.
Unused as they were to the appalling sounds, or the vivid flashes from the batteries, they stood for hours fascinated with horror.
After two days of bombing, the Union garrison surrendered. Captain Lee eventually earned the rank of Lieutenant General in the Confederate army. After the war, he became a planter in Mississippi. He served as a state senator and a college president before dying in 1908.

CH. 3

Samuel English: The Battle of the First Bull Run

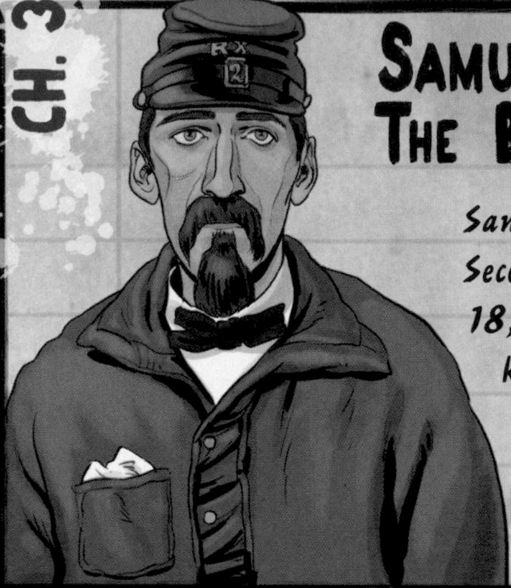

Samuel J. English was a corporal in Company D of the Second Rhode Island Volunteers. On the evening of July 18, 1861, Union troops made camp along a stream known as Bull Run, in Virginia. A short distance away, Confederate forces guarded an important railroad junction. The scene was set for the first major conflict of the Civil War.

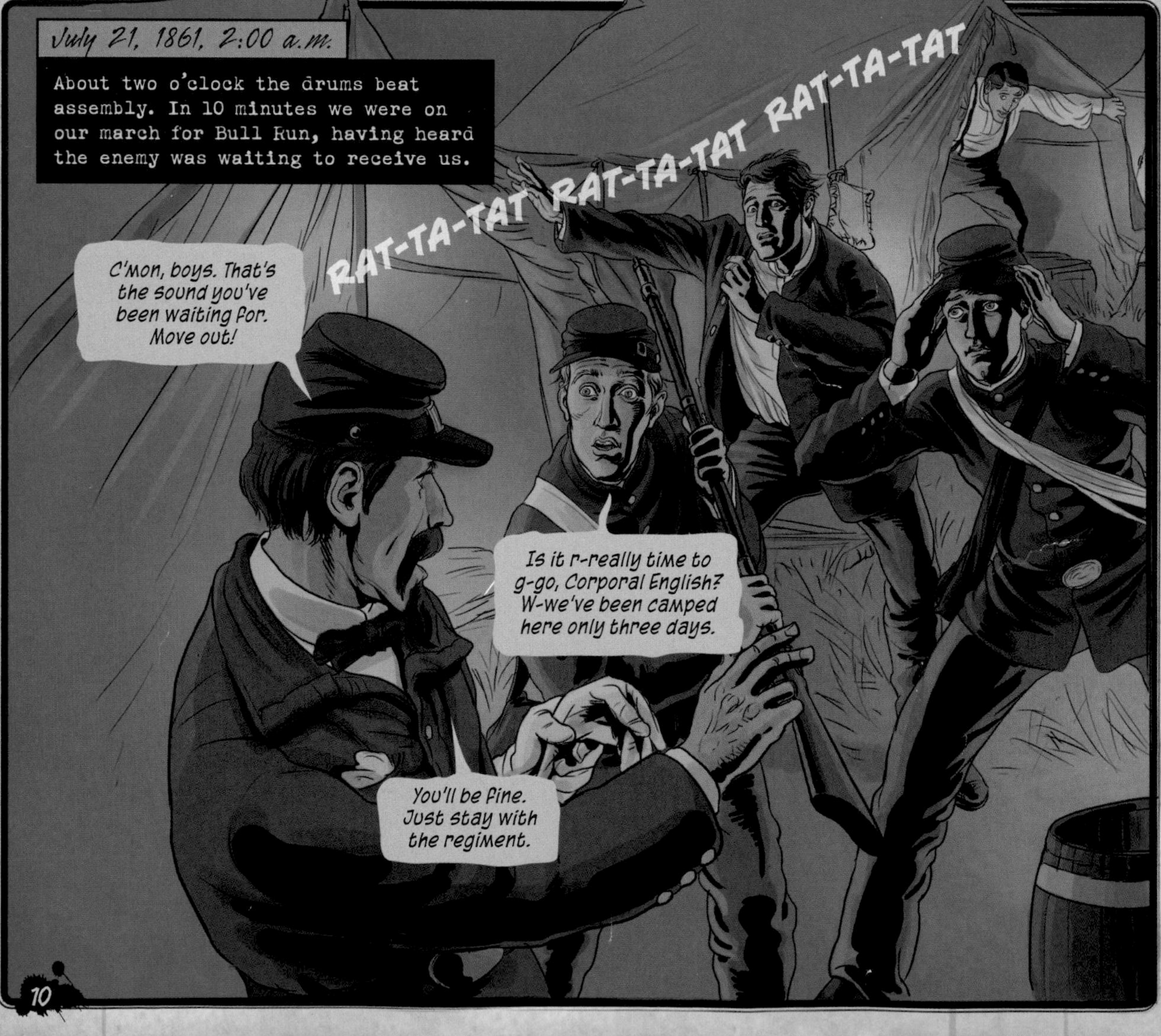
July 21, 1861, 2:00 a.m.
About two o'clock the drums beat assembly. In 10 minutes we were on our march for Bull Run, having heard the enemy was waiting to receive us.
RAT-TA-TAT RAT-TA-TAT RAT-TA-TAT RAT-TA-TAT
C'mon, boys. That's the sound you've been waiting for. Move out!
Is it r-really time to g-go, Corporal English? W-we've been camped here only three days.
You'll be fine. Just stay with the regiment.

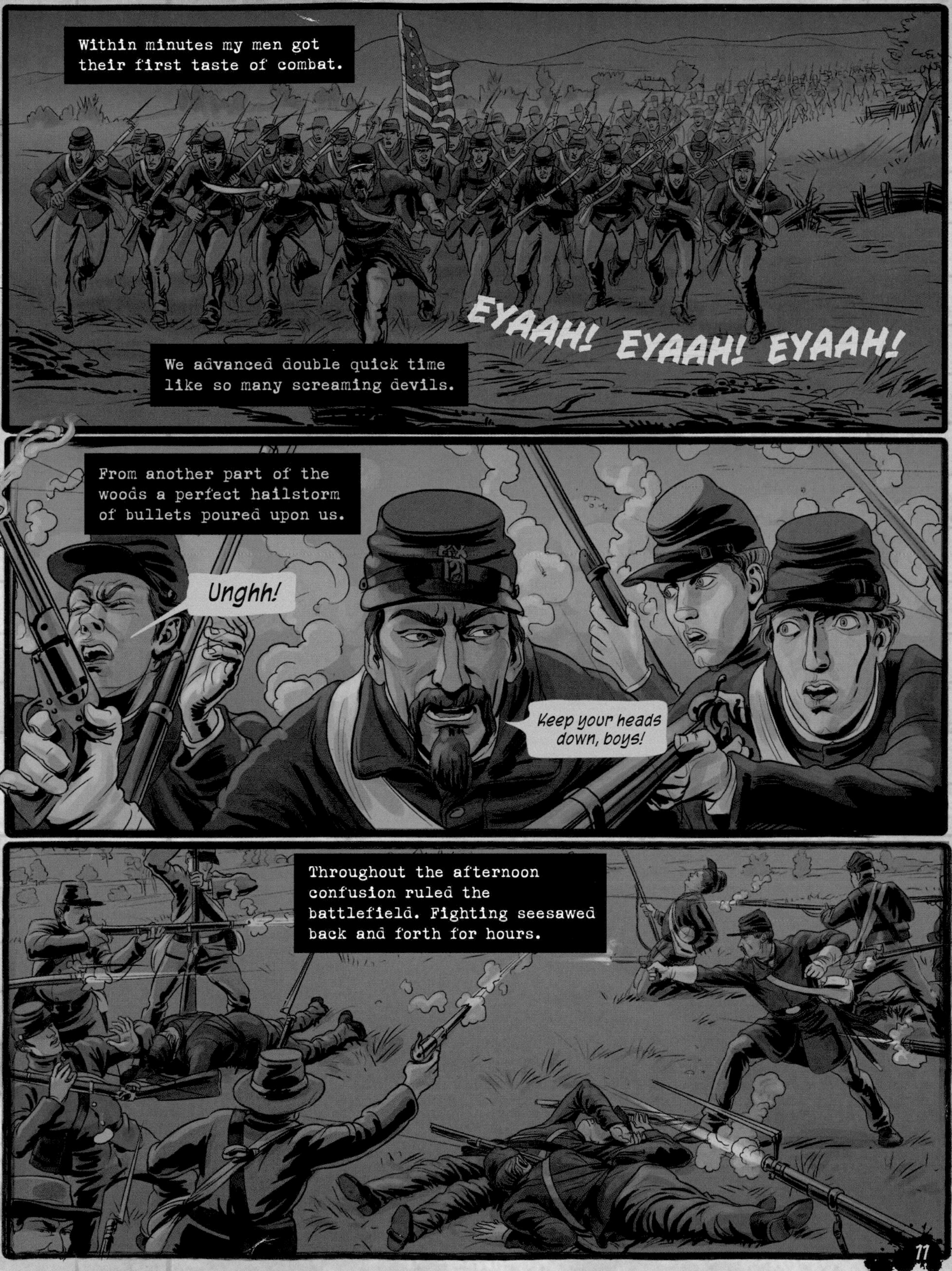
Within minutes my men got their first taste of combat.
EYAAH! EYAAH! EYAAH!
We advanced double quick time like so many screaming devils.
From another part of the woods a perfect hailstorm of bullets poured upon us.
Unghh!
Keep your heads down, boys!
Throughout the afternoon confusion ruled the battlefield. Fighting seesawed back and forth for hours.

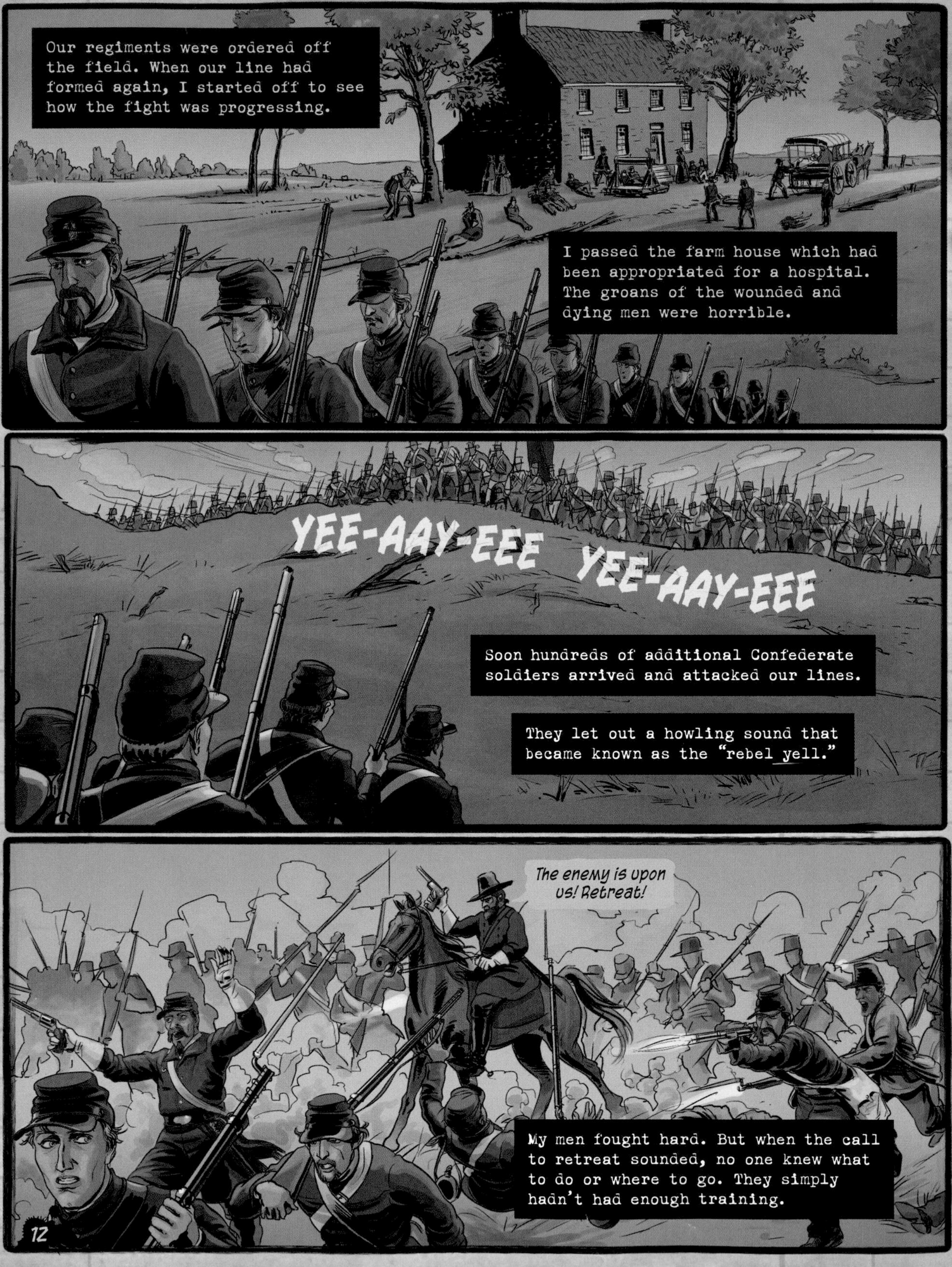
Our regiments were ordered off the field. When our line had formed again, I started off to see how the fight was progressing.
I passed the farm house which had been appropriated for a hospital. The groans of the wounded and dying men were horrible.
YEE-AAY-EEE
YEE-AAY-EEE
Soon hundreds of additional Confederate soldiers arrived and attacked our lines.
They let out a howling sound that became known as the "rebel yell."
The enemy is upon us! Retreat!
My men fought hard. But when the call to retreat sounded, no one knew what to do or where to go. They simply hadn't had enough training.

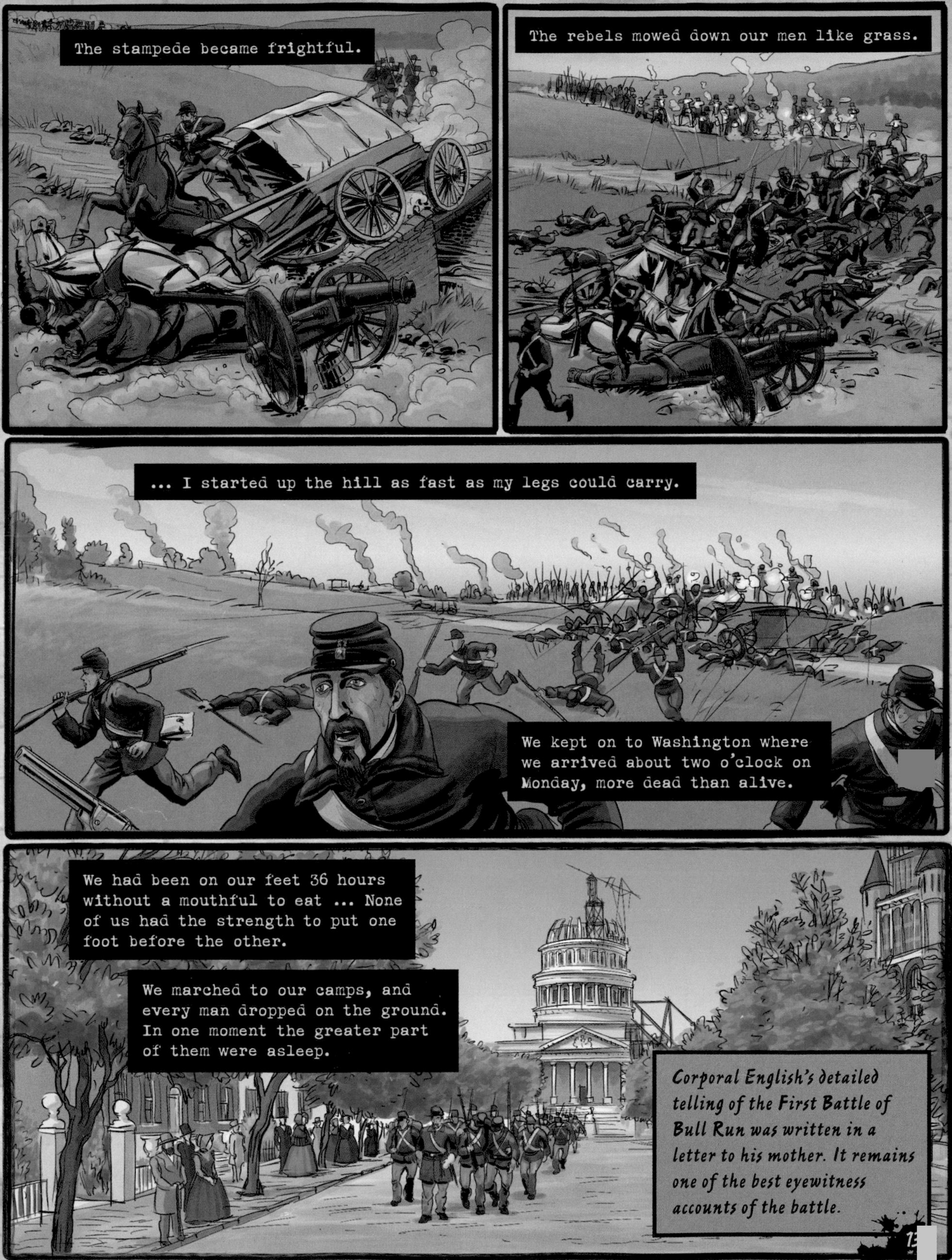
The stampede became frightful.
The rebels mowed down our men like grass.
... I started up the hill as fast as my legs could carry.
We kept on to Washington where we arrived about two o'clock on Monday, more dead than alive.
We had been on our feet 36 hours without a mouthful to eat ... None of us had the strength to put one foot before the other.
We marched to our camps, and every man dropped on the ground. In one moment the greater part of them were asleep.
Corporal English's detailed telling of the First Battle of Bull Run was written in a letter to his mother. It remains one of the best eyewitness accounts of the battle.

Samuel Dana Greene: Battle of the Ironclads

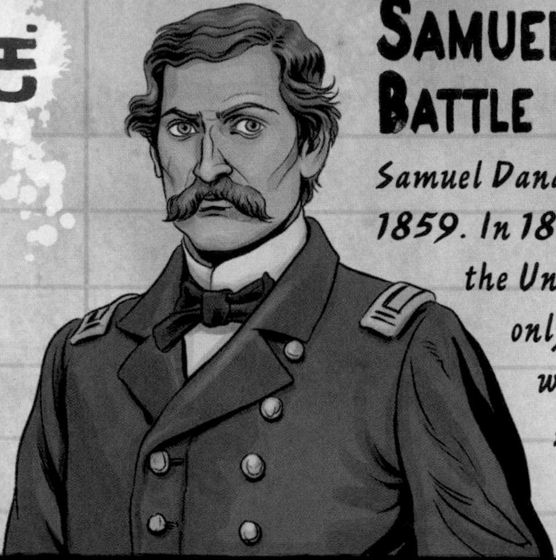

Samuel Dana Greene graduated from the U.S. Naval Academy in 1859. In 1862 he became executive officer of the USS Monitor, the Union's new ironclad ship. It was the navy's last and only hope against the Confederate ironclad Merrimac, which had recently begun destroying Union wooden ships. If Greene and the Monitor couldn't stop the Merrimac, the Union navy would be doomed.

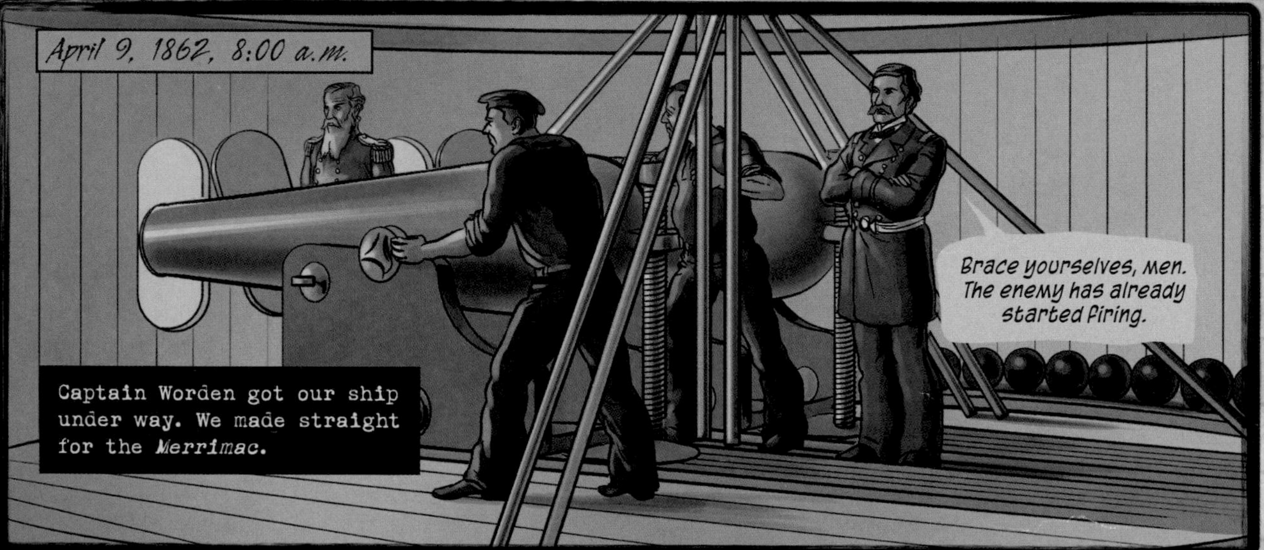

April 9, 1862, 8:00 a.m.
Brace yourselves, men. The enemy has already started firing.
Captain Worden got our ship under way. We made straight for the Merrimac.

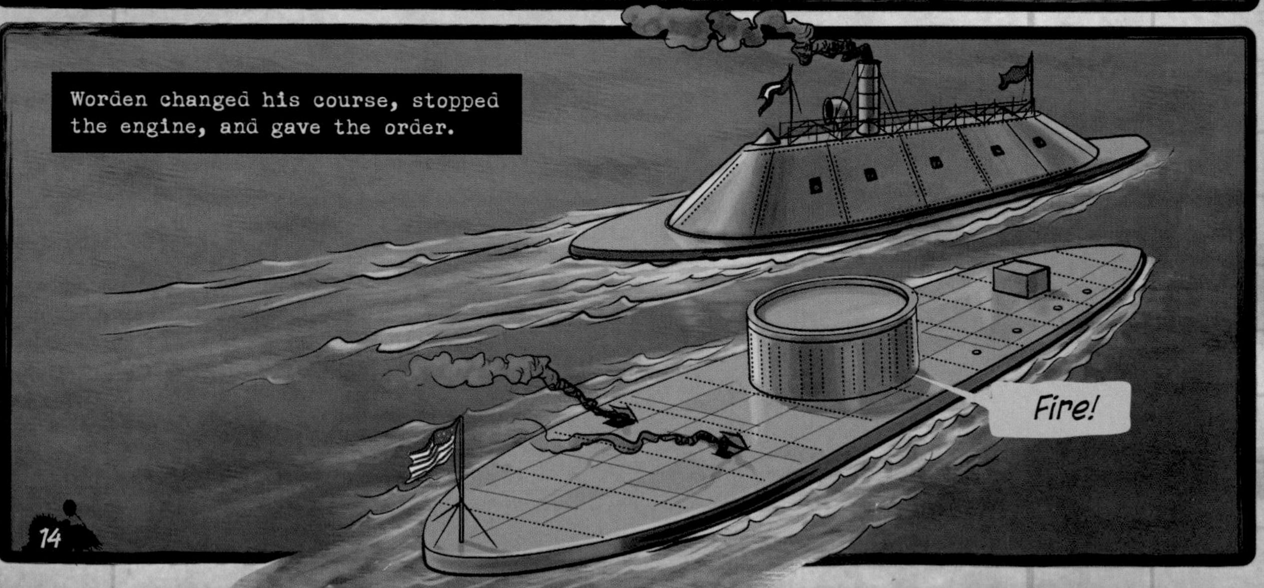

Worden changed his course, stopped the engine, and gave the order.
Fire!

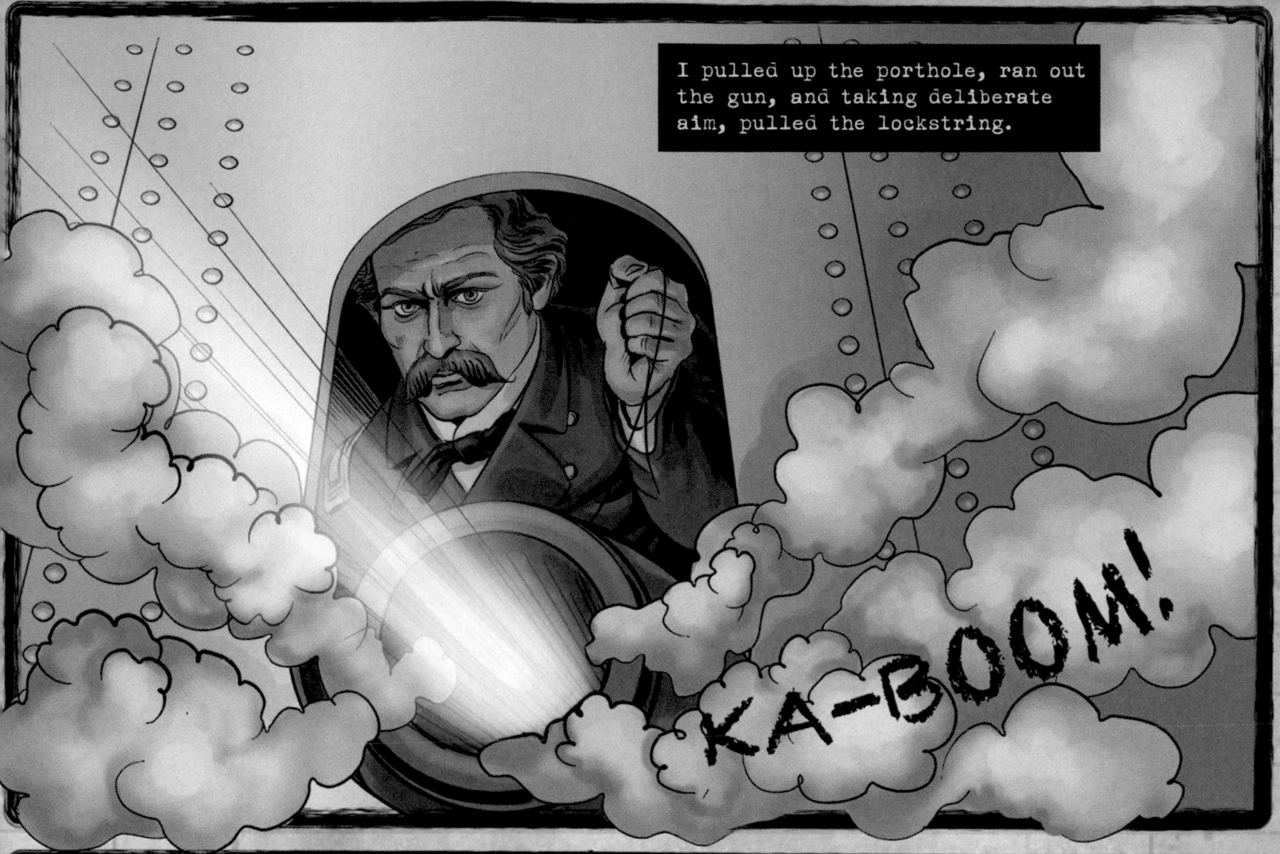
I pulled up the porthole, ran out the gun, and taking deliberate aim, pulled the lockstring.
KA-BOOM!

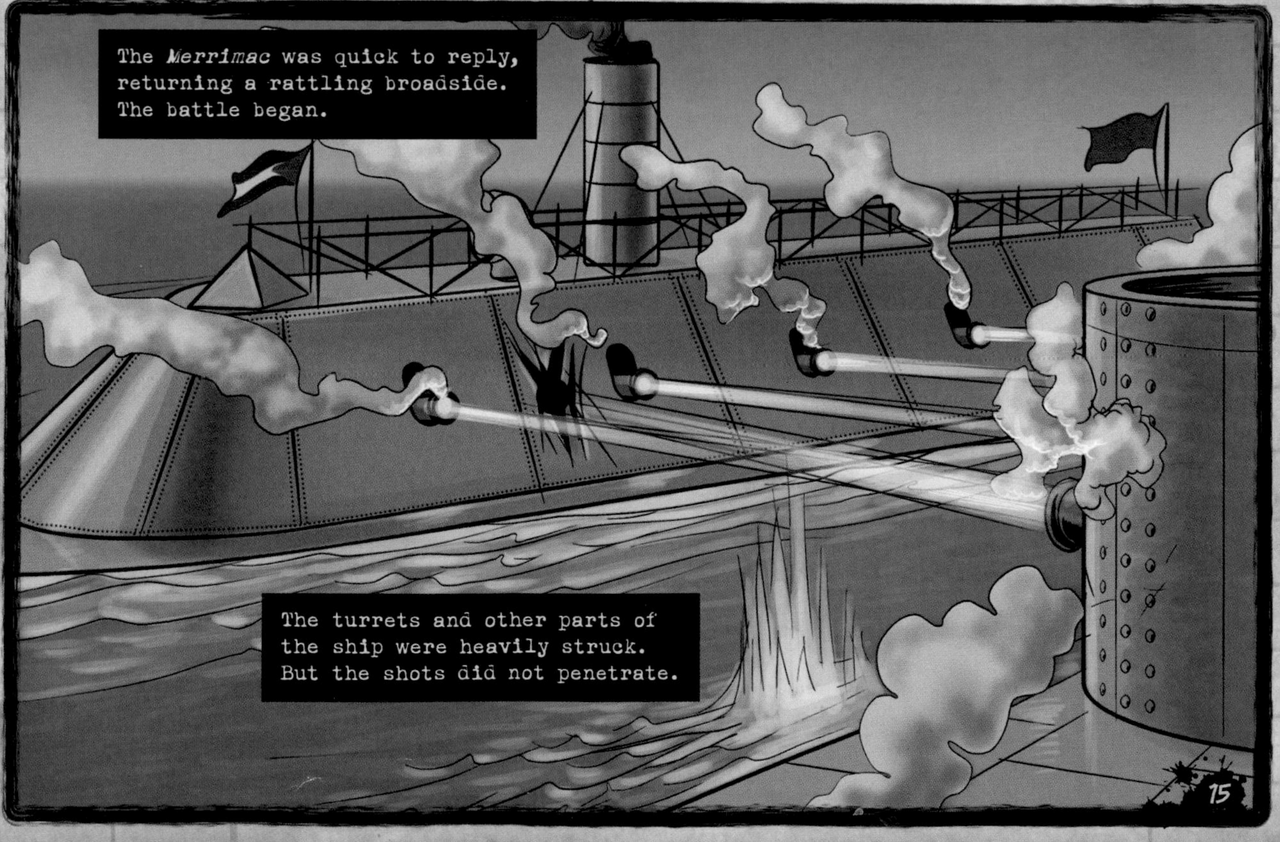
The *Merrimac* was quick to reply, returning a rattling broadside. The battle began.
The turrets and other parts of the ship were heavily struck. But the shots did not penetrate.

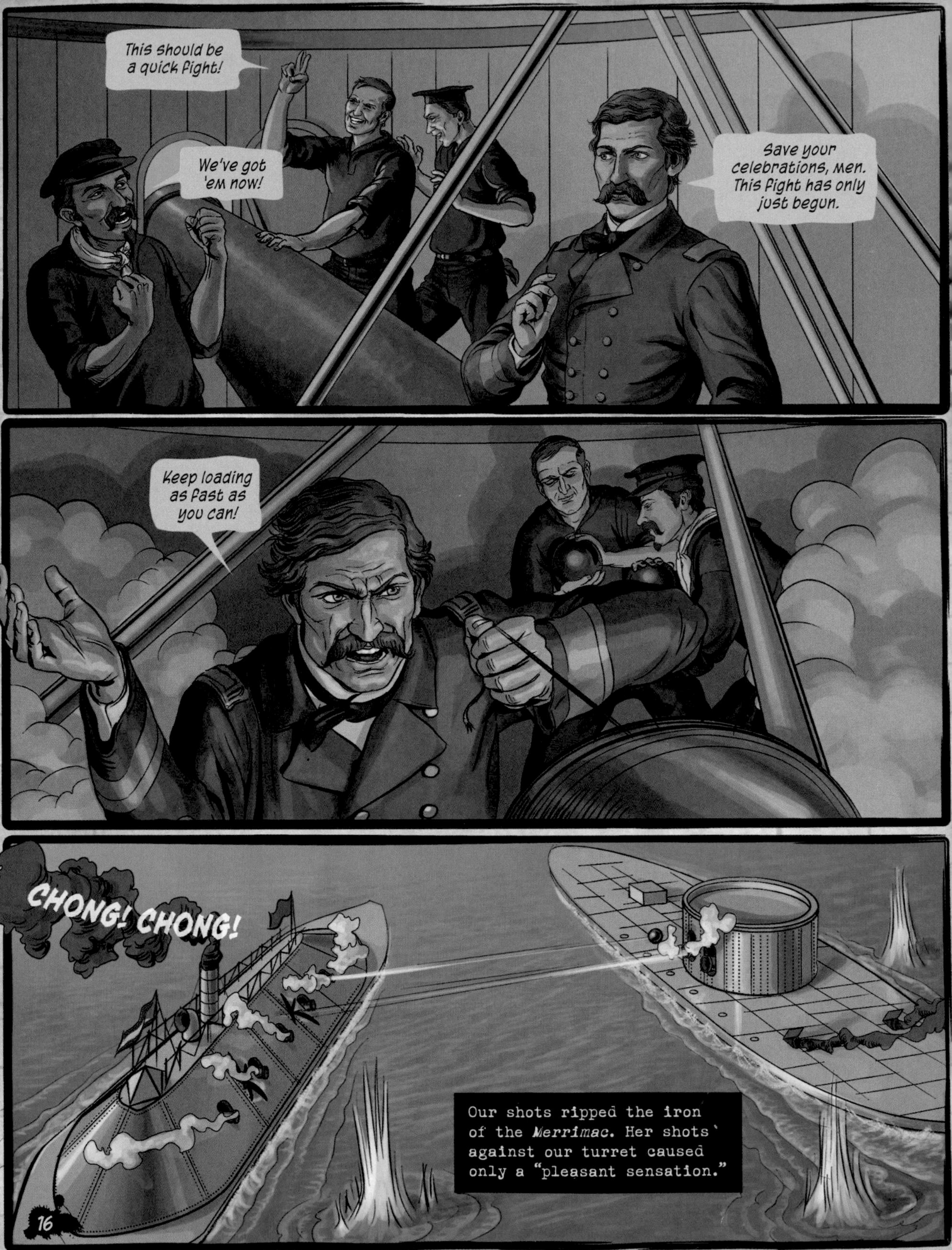
This should be a quick fight!
We've got 'em now!
Save your celebrations, men. This fight has only just begun.
Keep loading as fast as you can!
CHONG! CHONG!
Our shots ripped the iron of the *Merrimac*. Her shots against our turret caused only a "pleasant sensation."

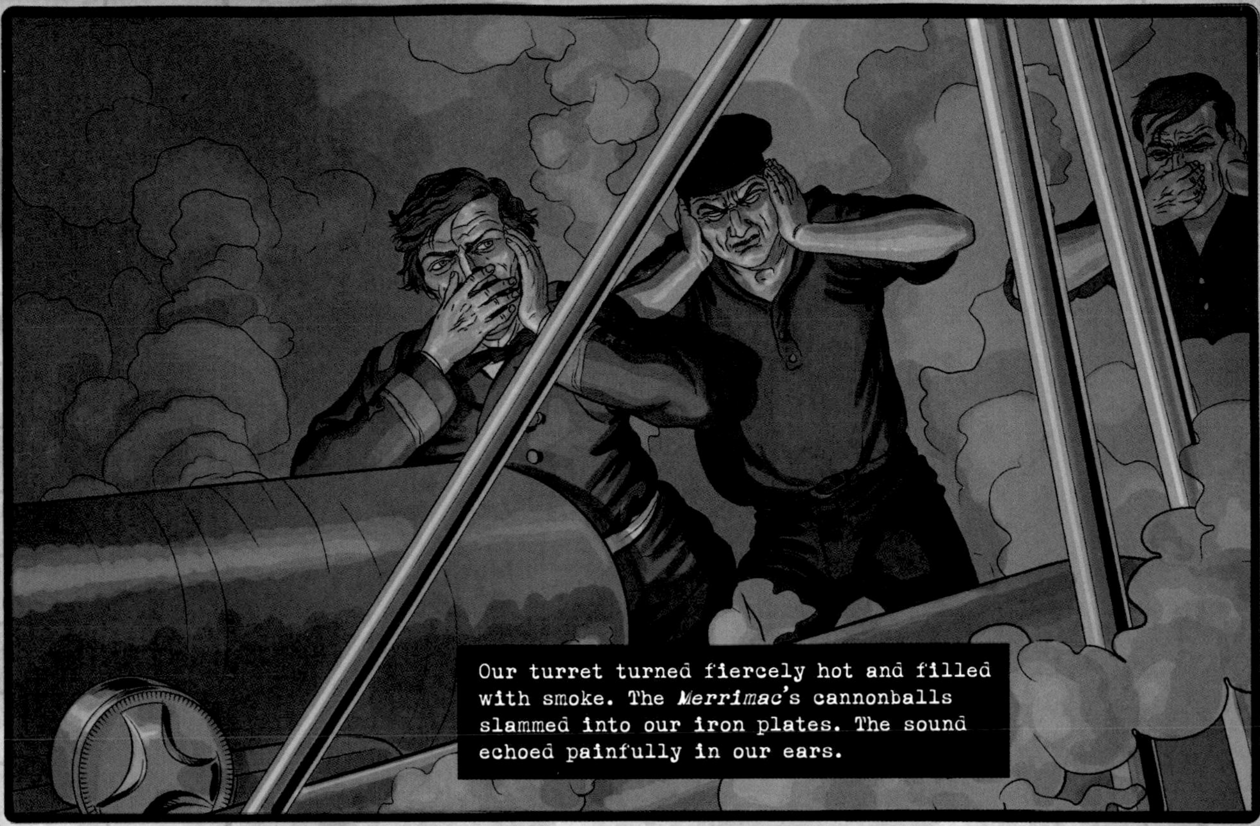
Our turret turned fiercely hot and filled with smoke. The *Merrimac*'s cannonballs slammed into our iron plates. The sound echoed painfully in our ears.

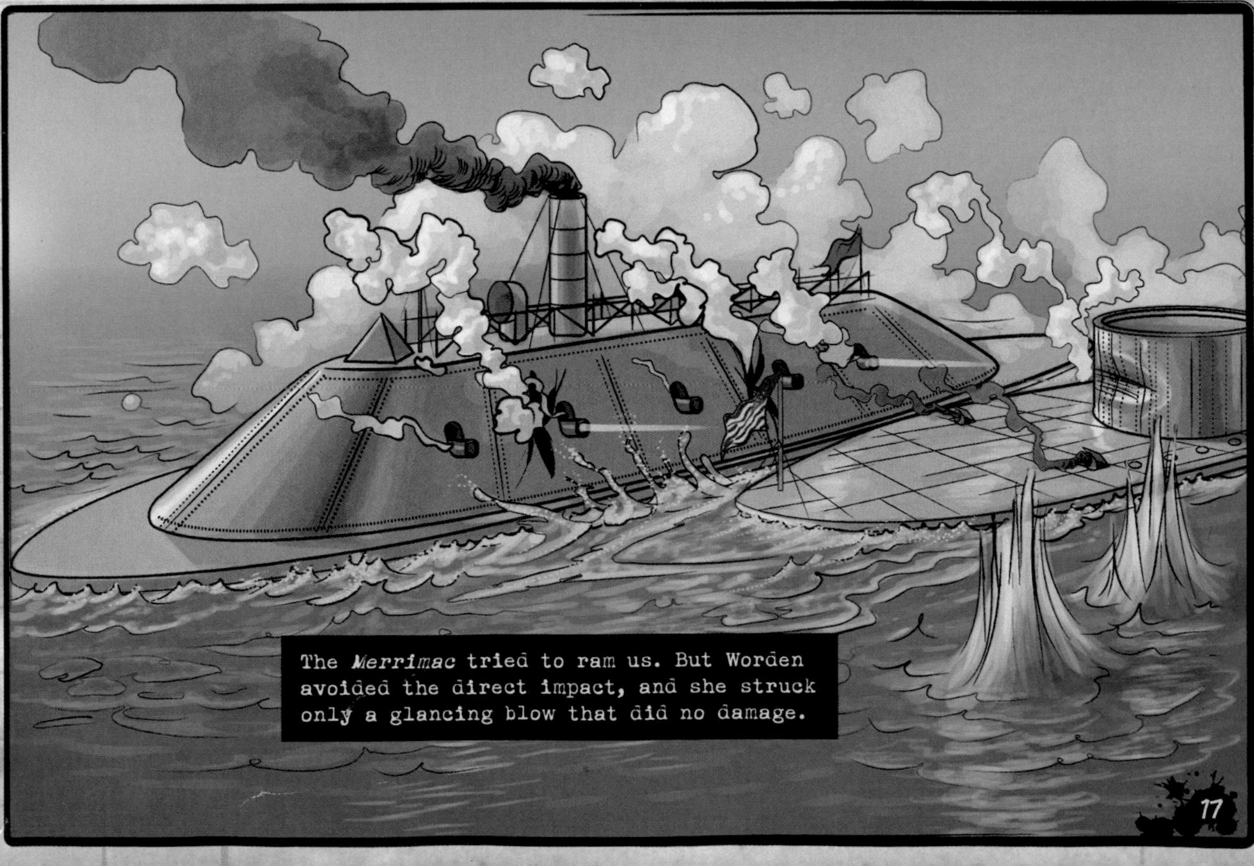
The *Merrimac* tried to ram us. But Worden avoided the direct impact, and she struck only a glancing blow that did no damage.

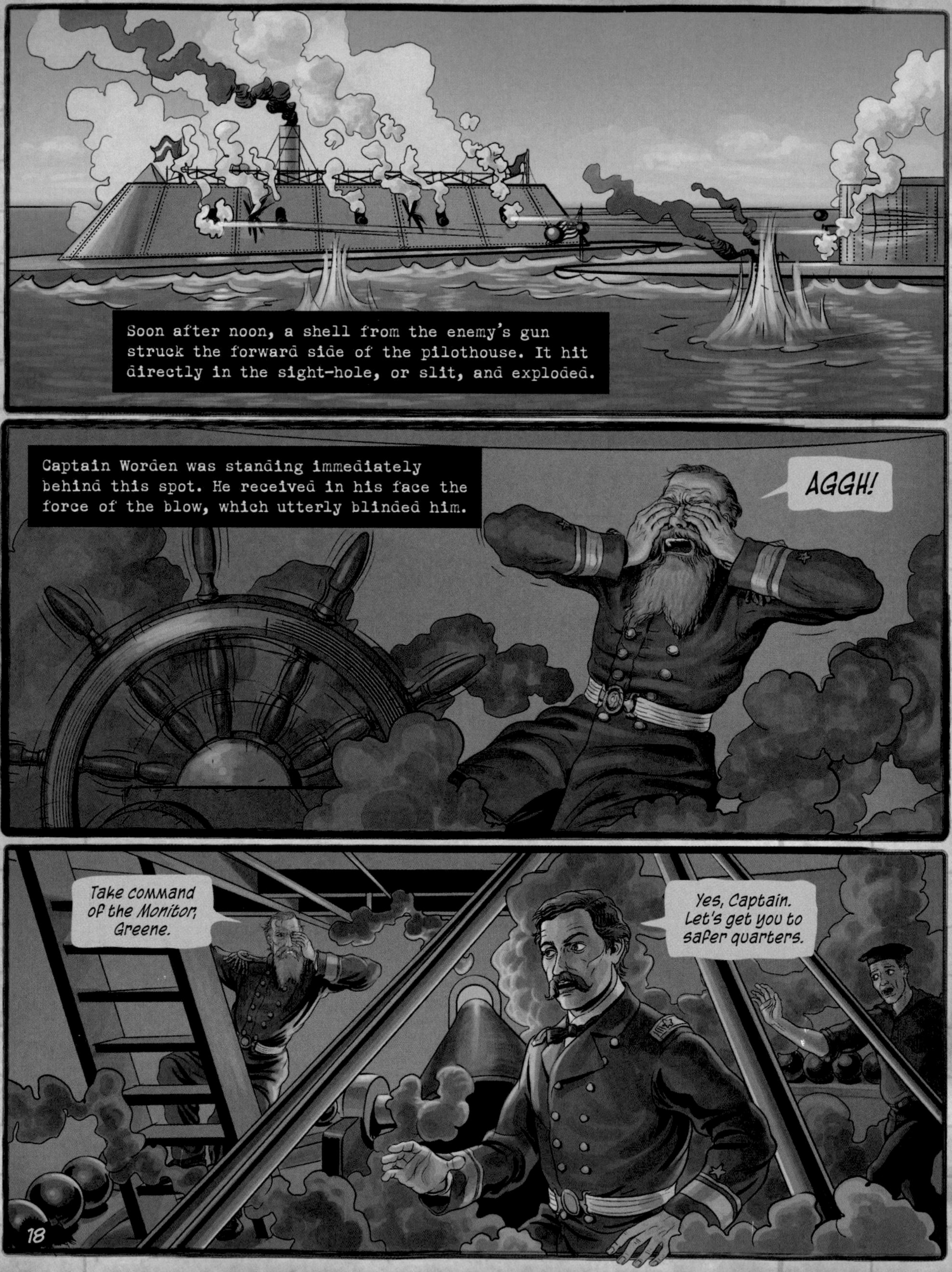
Soon after noon, a shell from the enemy's gun struck the forward side of the pilothouse. It hit directly in the sight-hole, or slit, and exploded.
Captain Worden was standing immediately behind this spot. He received in his face the force of the blow, which utterly blinded him.
AGGH!
Take command of the Monitor, Greene.
Yes, Captain. Let's get you to safer quarters.

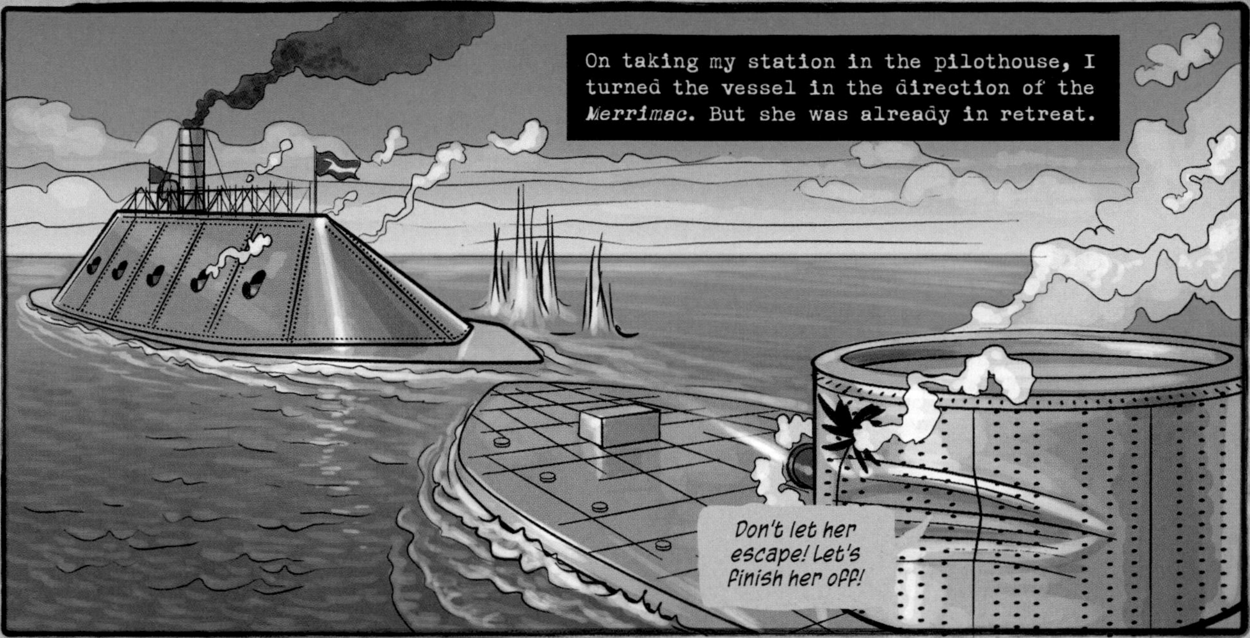
On taking my station in the pilothouse, I turned the vessel in the direction of the *Merrimac*. But she was already in retreat.
Don't let her escape! Let's finish her off!

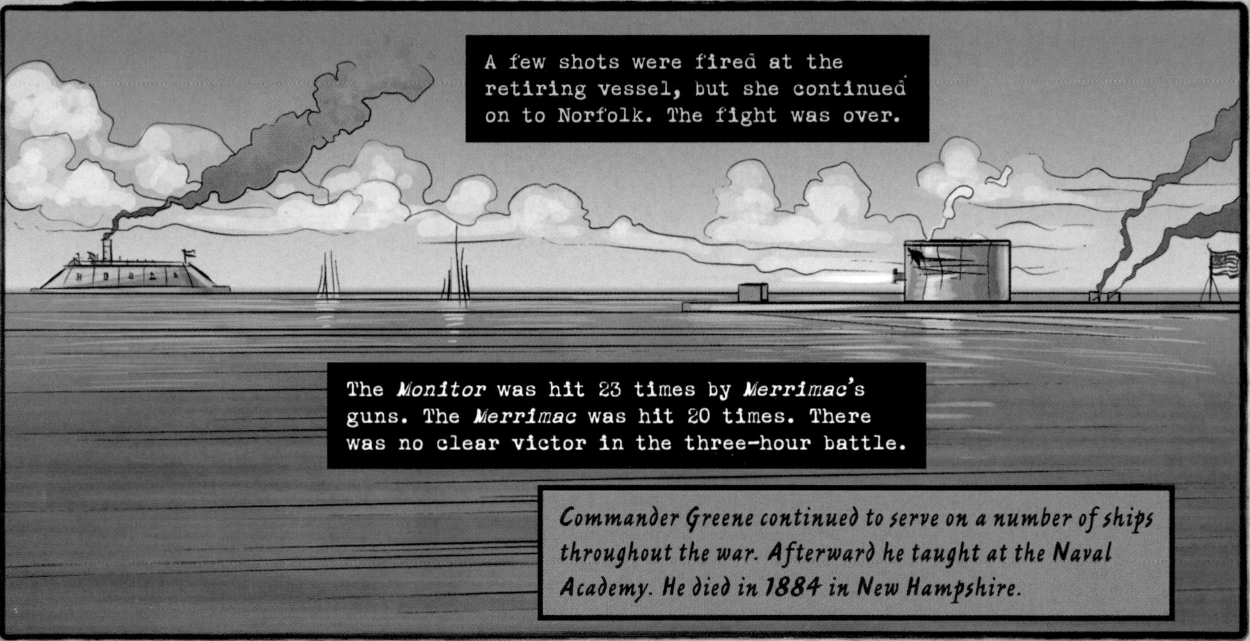
A few shots were fired at the retiring vessel, but she continued on to Norfolk. The fight was over.
The *Monitor* was hit 23 times by *Merrimac*'s guns. The *Merrimac* was hit 20 times. There was no clear victor in the three-hour battle.
Commander Greene continued to serve on a number of ships throughout the war. Afterward he taught at the Naval Academy. He died in 1884 in New Hampshire.

COMPARING GUNS

The USS Monitor *had a spinning turret that allowed it to fire its two cannons in almost any direction. The* Merrimac's *10 guns, on the other hand, were set in place and couldn't be moved.*

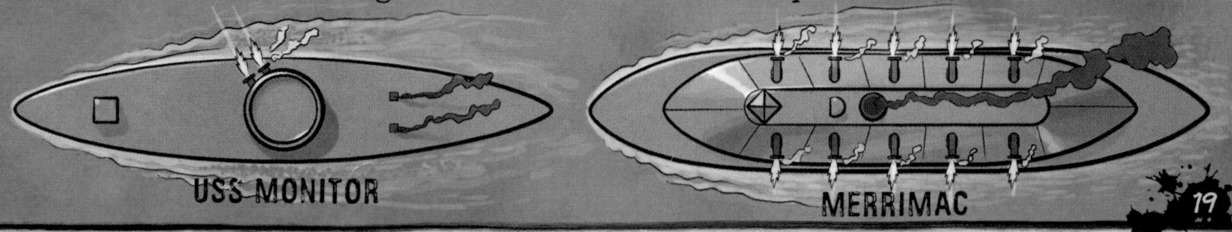
USS MONITOR
MERRIMAC

David Thompson: The Battle of Antietam

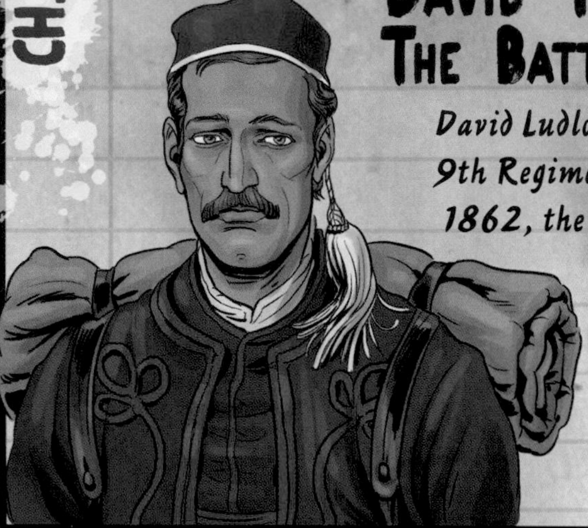

David Ludlow Thompson was a private in Company G, 9th Regiment, New York Volunteers. On September 17, 1862, the opening shots of the Battle of Antietam, in Maryland, were fired. A bloody struggle followed. It started in Miller's cornfield and ended at the Stone Bridge over Antietam Creek. Private Thompson and his regiment were positioned there.

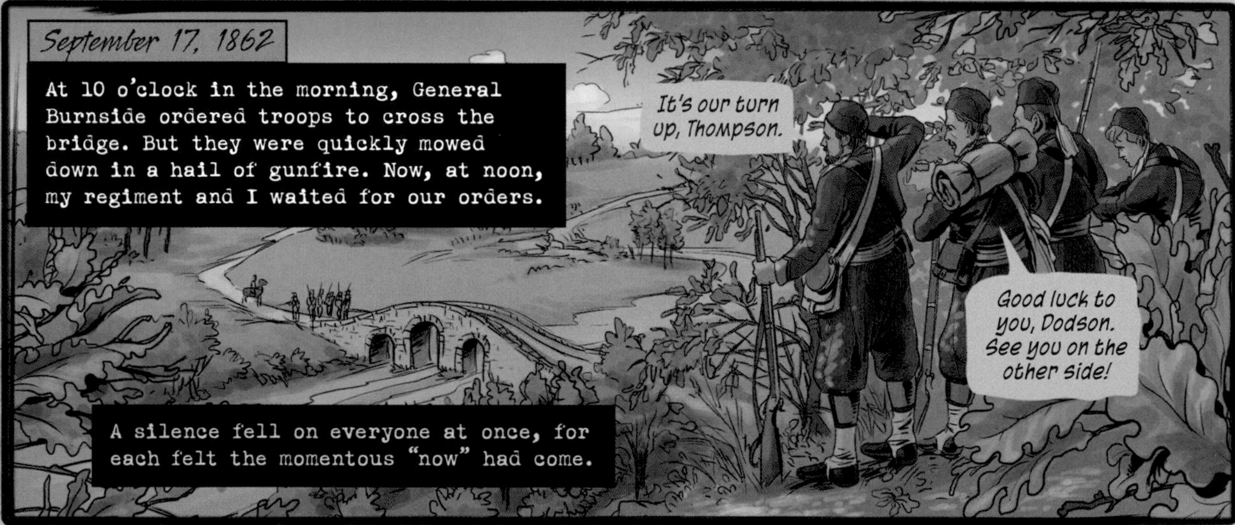
September 17, 1862
At 10 o'clock in the morning, General Burnside ordered troops to cross the bridge. But they were quickly mowed down in a hail of gunfire. Now, at noon, my regiment and I waited for our orders.
It's our turn up, Thompson.
Good luck to you, Dodson. See you on the other side!
A silence fell on everyone at once, for each felt the momentous "now" had come.

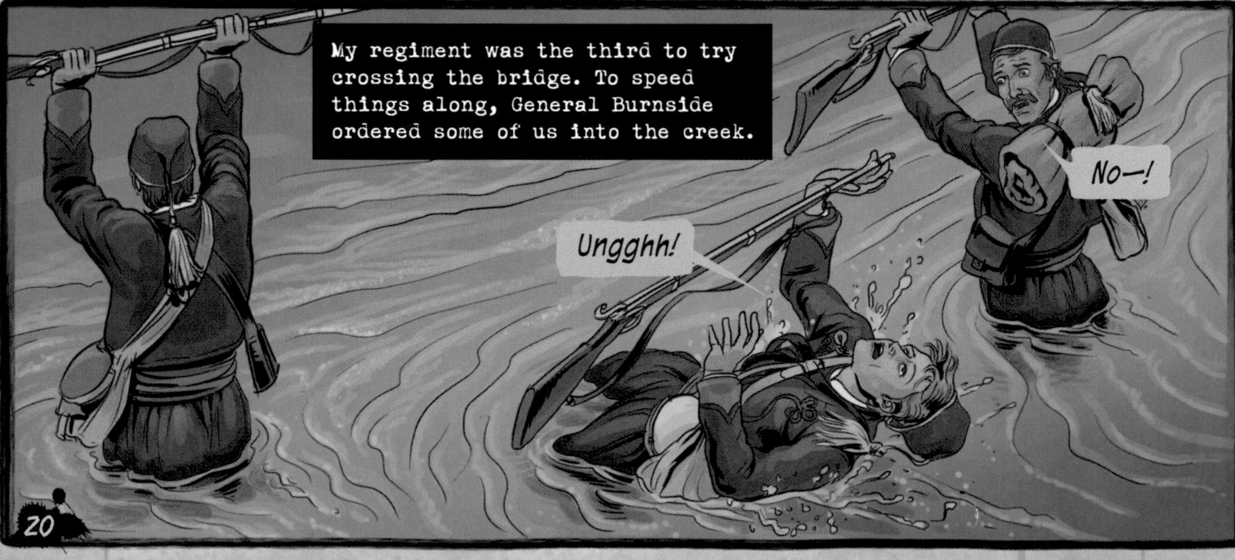
My regiment was the third to try crossing the bridge. To speed things along, General Burnside ordered some of us into the creek.
No—!
Ungghh!

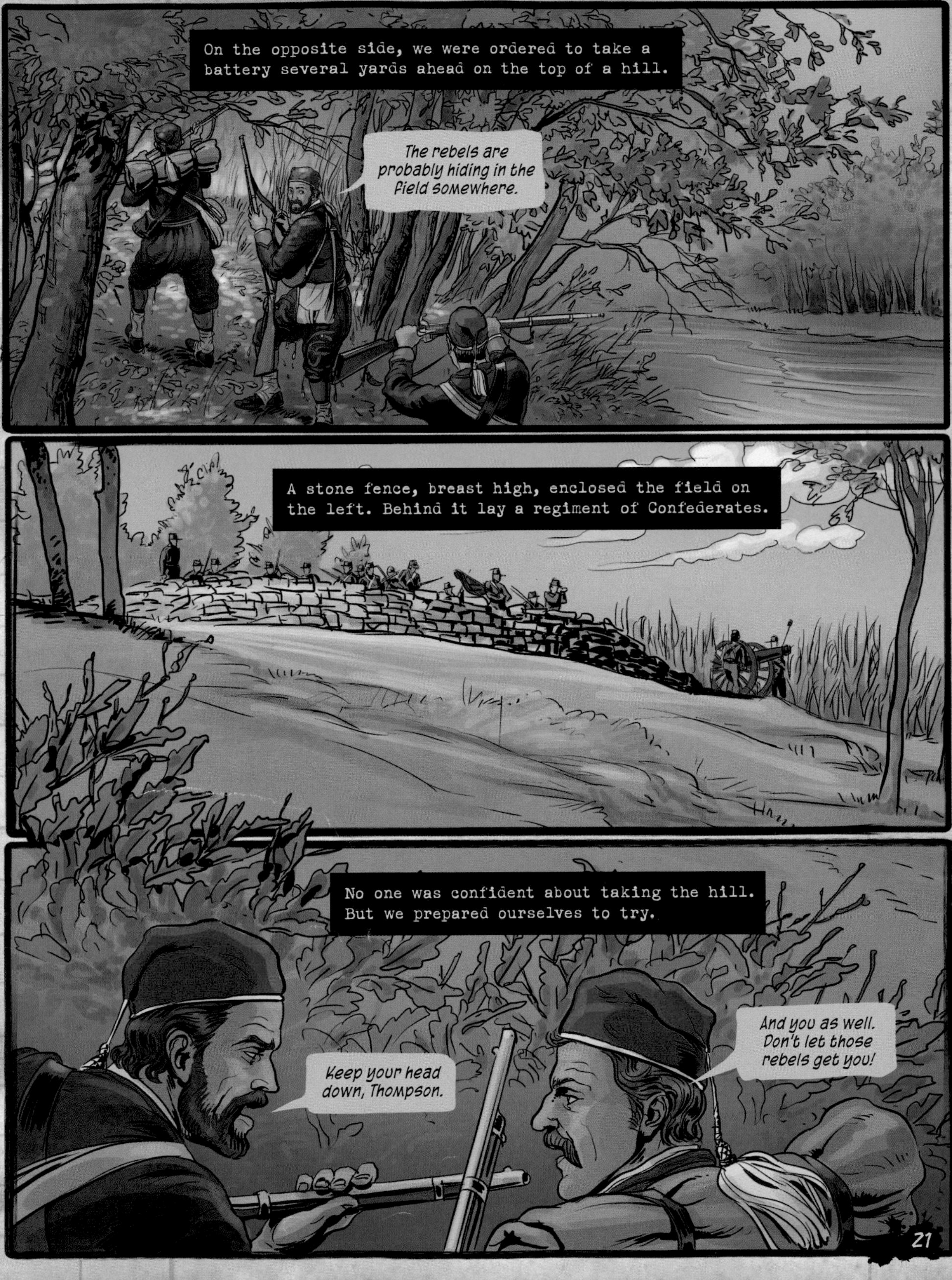
On the opposite side, we were ordered to take a battery several yards ahead on the top of a hill.
The rebels are probably hiding in the field somewhere.
A stone fence, breast high, enclosed the field on the left. Behind it lay a regiment of Confederates.
No one was confident about taking the hill. But we prepared ourselves to try.
Keep your head down, Thompson.
And you as well. Don't let those rebels get you!

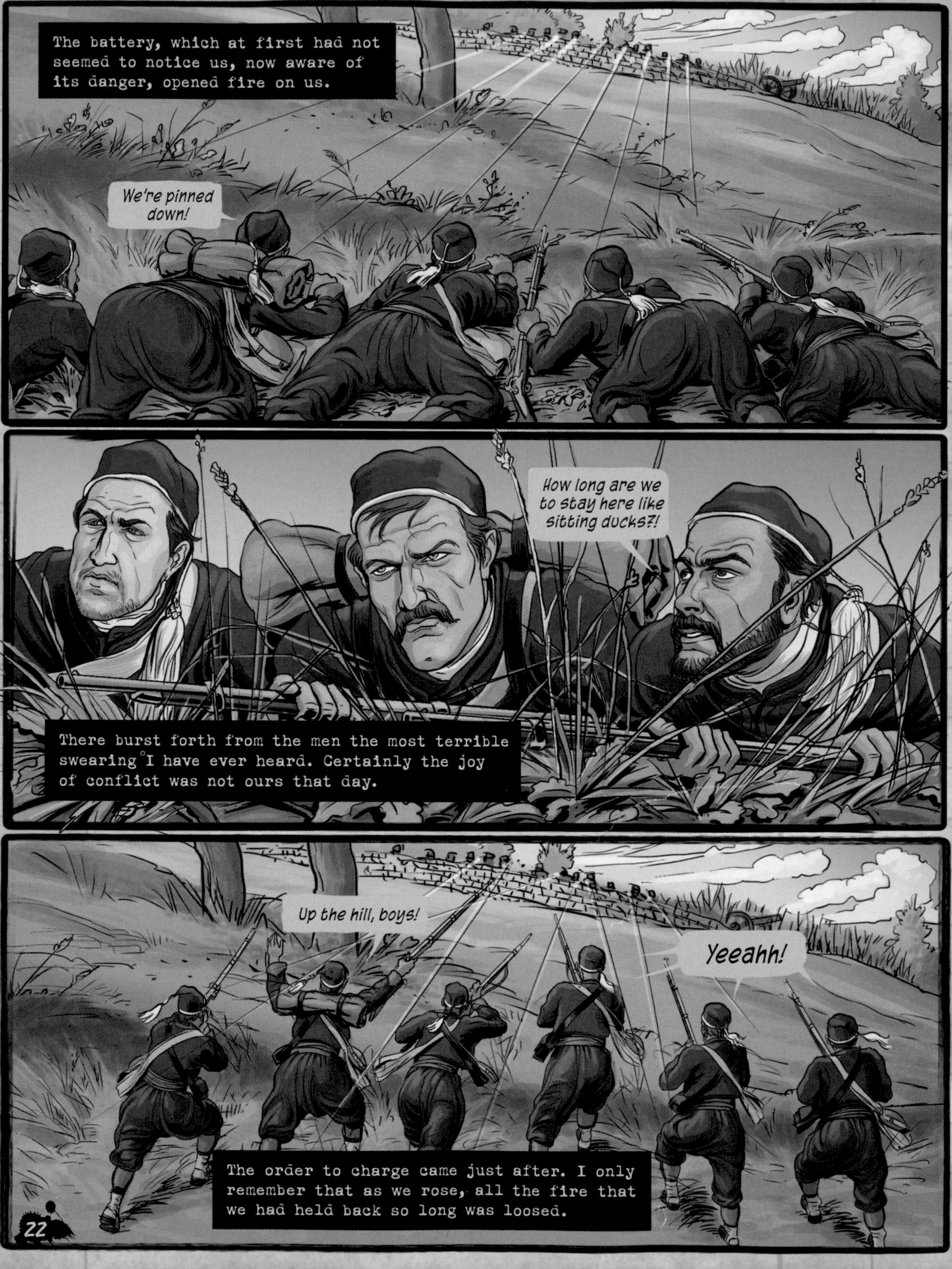
The battery, which at first had not seemed to notice us, now aware of its danger, opened fire on us.
We're pinned down!
How long are we to stay here like sitting ducks?!
There burst forth from the men the most terrible swearing I have ever heard. Certainly the joy of conflict was not ours that day.
Up the hill, boys!
Yeeahh!
The order to charge came just after. I only remember that as we rose, all the fire that we had held back so long was loosed.

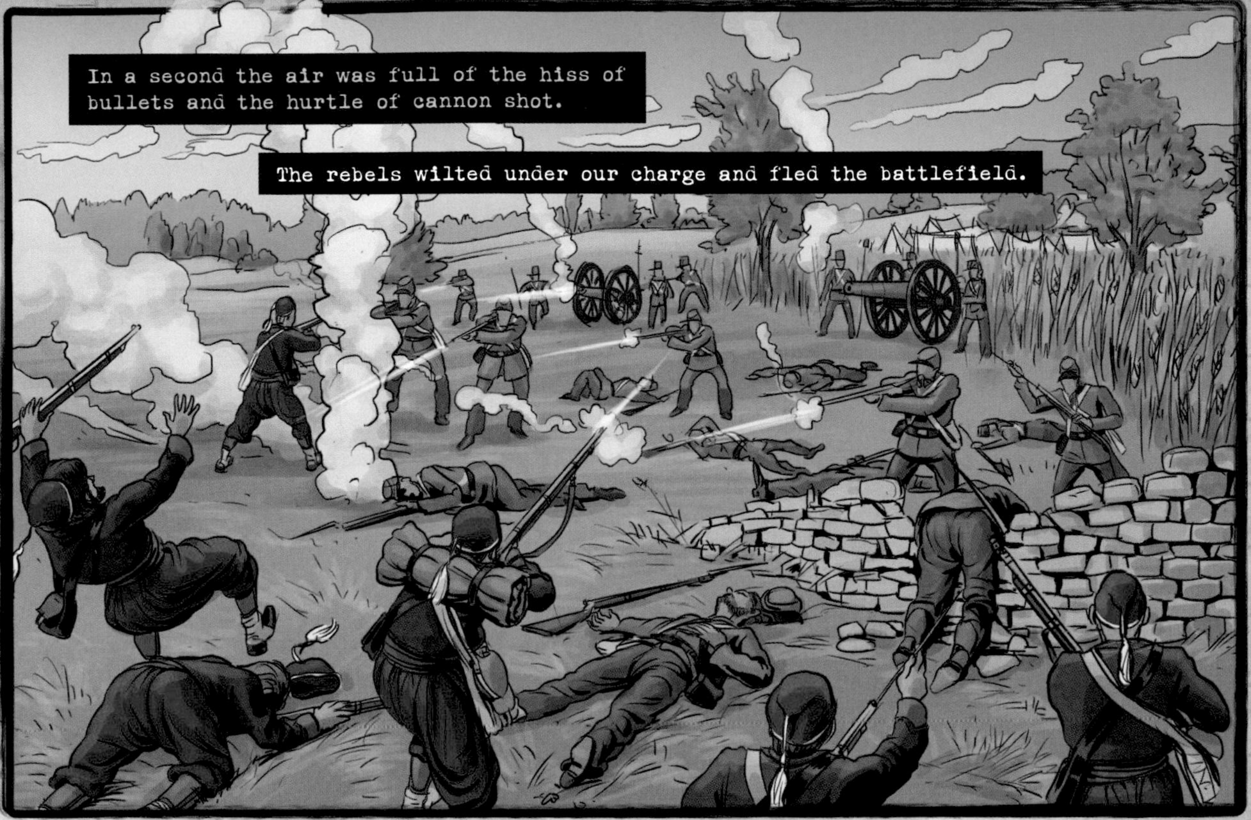
In a second the air was full of the hiss of bullets and the hurtle of cannon shot.
The rebels wilted under our charge and fled the battlefield.

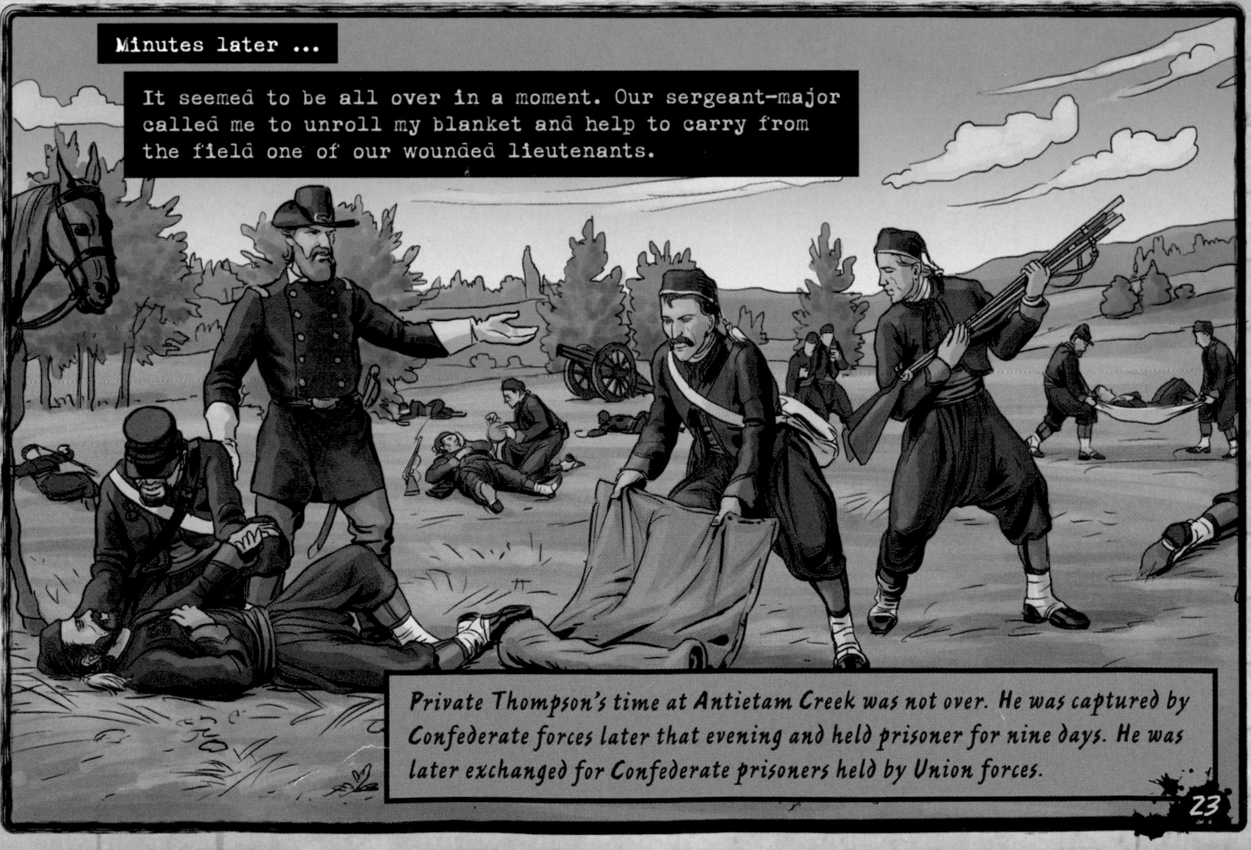
Minutes later ...
It seemed to be all over in a moment. Our sergeant-major called me to unroll my blanket and help to carry from the field one of our wounded lieutenants.
Private Thompson's time at Antietam Creek was not over. He was captured by Confederate forces later that evening and held prisoner for nine days. He was later exchanged for Confederate prisoners held by Union forces.

General James Longstreet: The Battle of Gettysburg

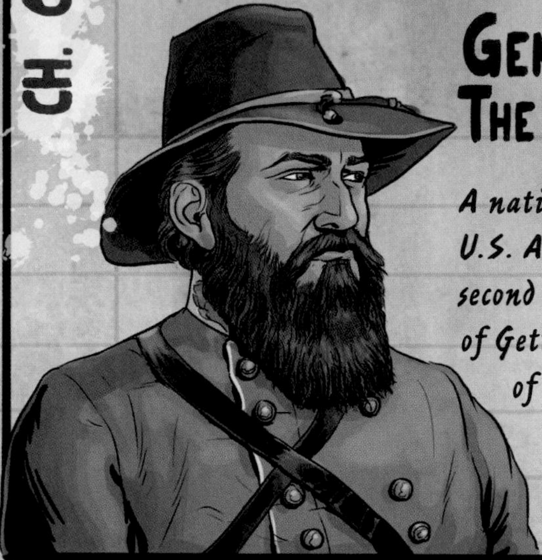

A native Southerner, General James Longstreet quit the U.S. Army in 1861 and joined the Confederacy. He was second in command to General Robert E. Lee at the Battle of Gettysburg in Pennsylvania. On the third and final day of fighting, Lee planned to charge the center of the Union line. Longstreet strongly disagreed with the plan. He thought it would surely fail.

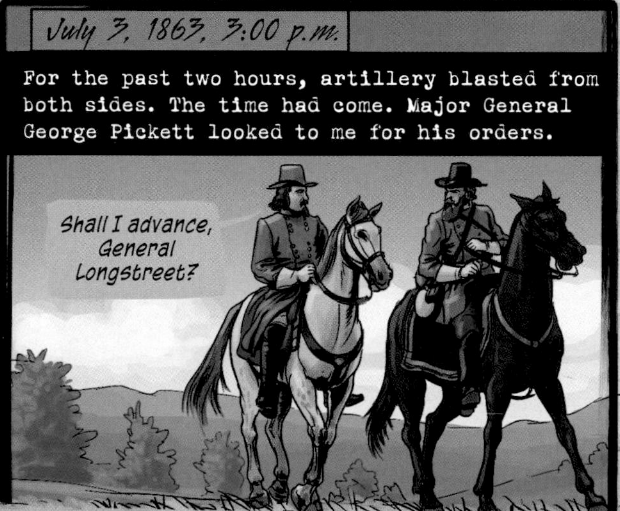
July 3, 1863, 3:00 p.m.
For the past two hours, artillery blasted from both sides. The time had come. Major General George Pickett looked to me for his orders.
Shall I advance, General Longstreet?

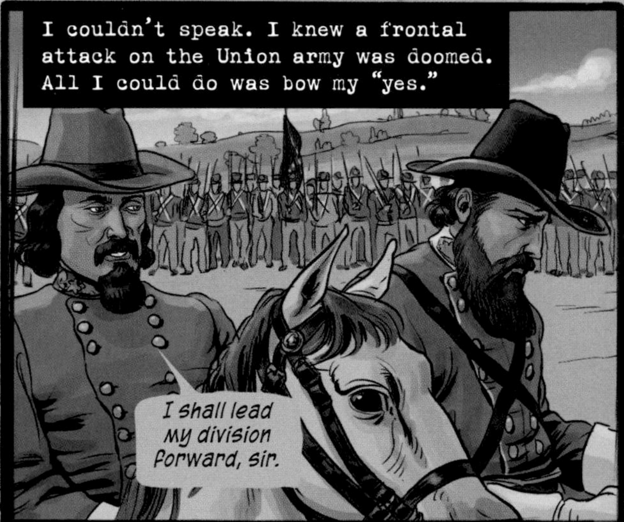
I couldn't speak. I knew a frontal attack on the Union army was doomed. All I could do was bow my "yes."
I shall lead my division forward, sir.

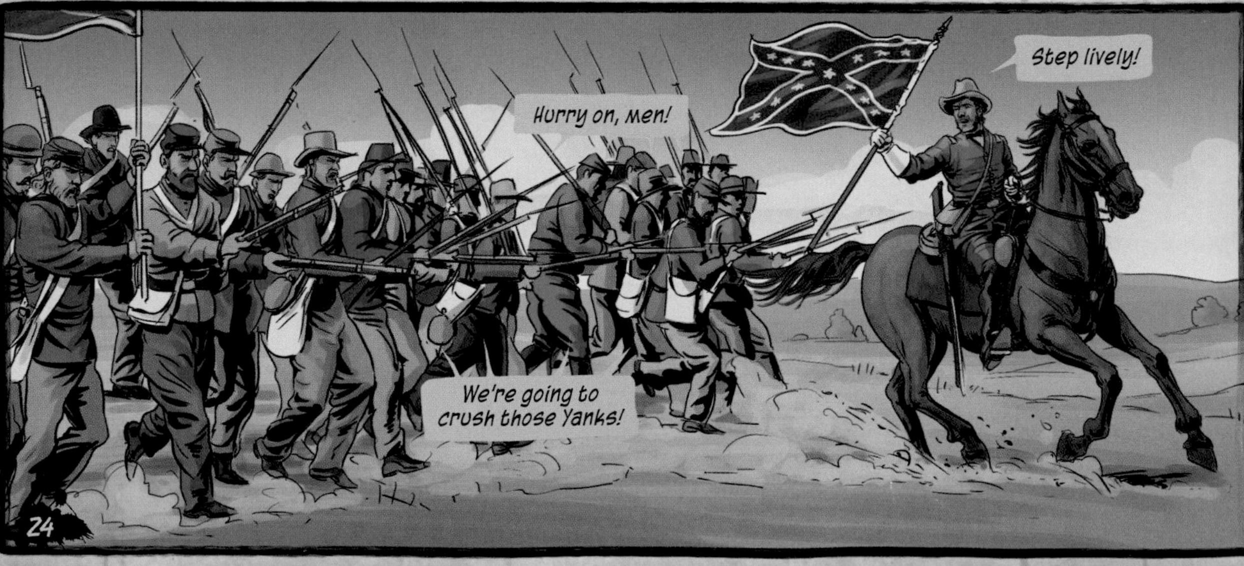
Hurry on, Men!
Step lively!
We're going to crush those Yanks!

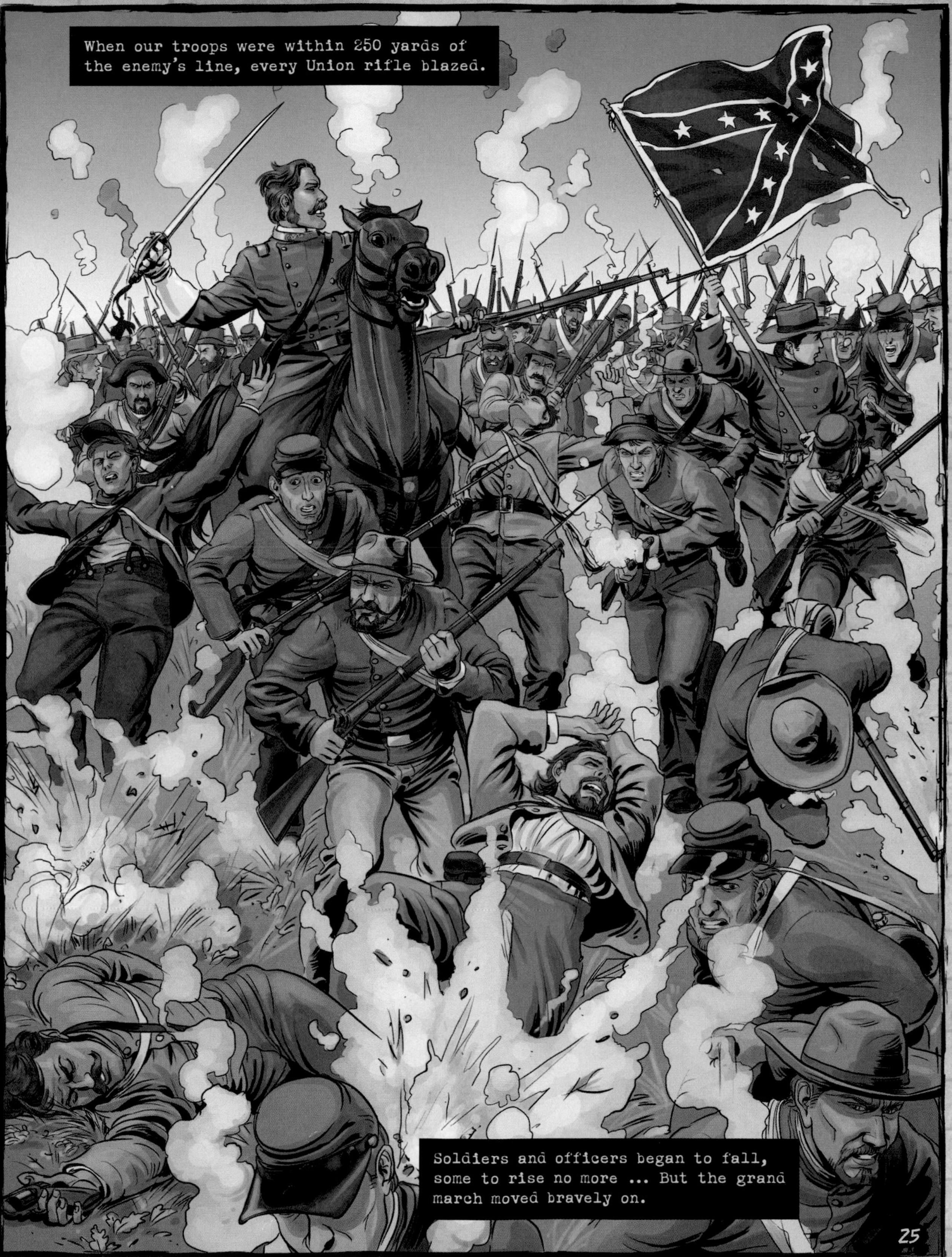
When our troops were within 250 yards of the enemy's line, every Union rifle blazed.
Soldiers and officers began to fall, some to rise no more ... But the grand march moved bravely on.

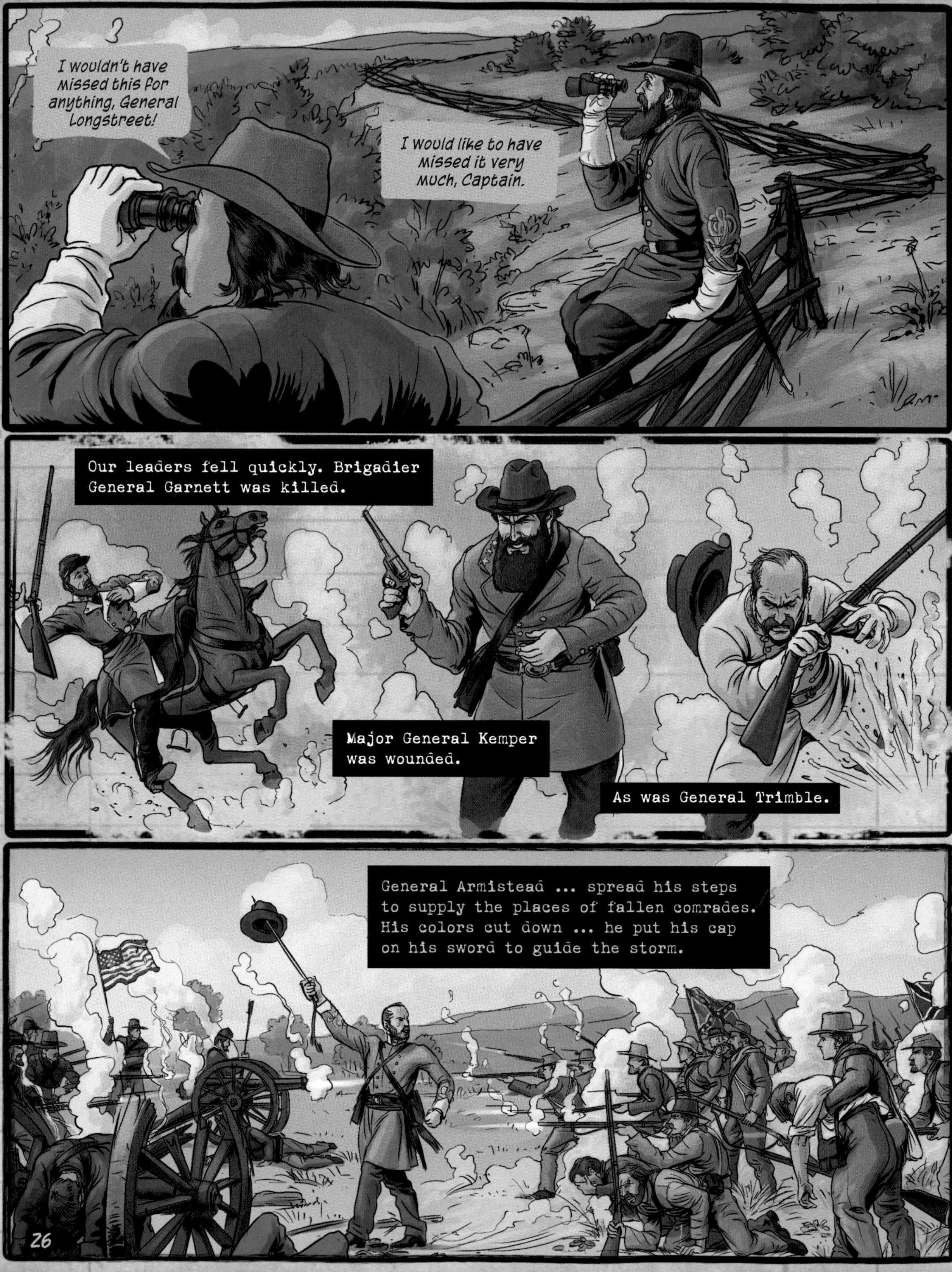
I wouldn't have missed this for anything, General Longstreet!
I would like to have missed it very much, Captain.
Our leaders fell quickly. Brigadier General Garnett was killed.
Major General Kemper was wounded.
As was General Trimble.
General Armistead ... spread his steps to supply the places of fallen comrades. His colors cut down ... he put his cap on his sword to guide the storm.

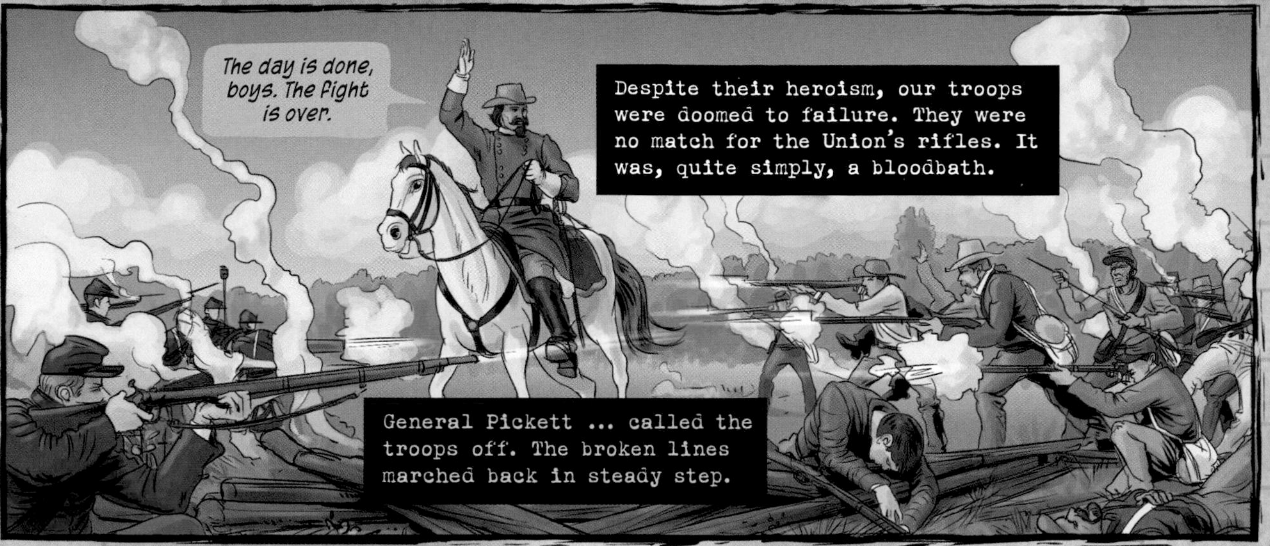
The day is done, boys. The fight is over.
Despite their heroism, our troops were doomed to failure. They were no match for the Union's rifles. It was, quite simply, a bloodbath.
General Pickett ... called the troops off. The broken lines marched back in steady step.

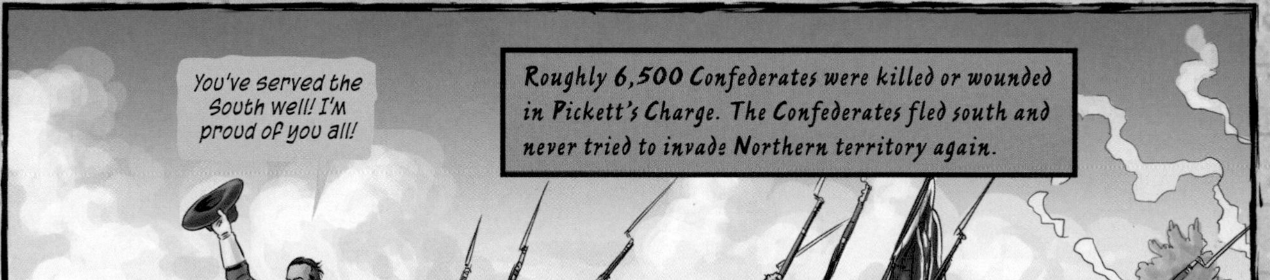
You've served the South well! I'm proud of you all!
Roughly 6,500 Confederates were killed or wounded in Pickett's Charge. The Confederates fled south and never tried to invade Northern territory again.
General Longstreet continued to serve as General Lee's "old war-horse" until the end of the war. He later worked for the U.S. government and wrote a memoir of his battle experiences. He lived to the age of 82.

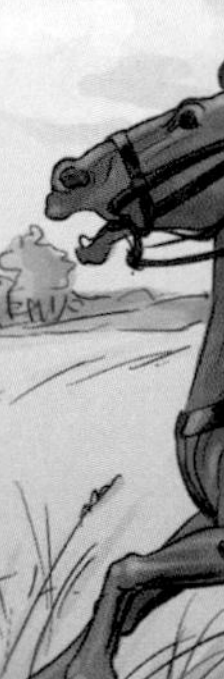

WOMEN SOLDIERS

Most women helped the war effort by providing supplies and offering whatever support they could. A few women, however, hid their true selves in order to serve in the Union and Confederate armies. They often cut their hair short and wore men's clothing when they went to sign up. Some women avoided the official process and joined a unit right before a battle.

CH. 7

General John Gordon: Surrender at Appomattox

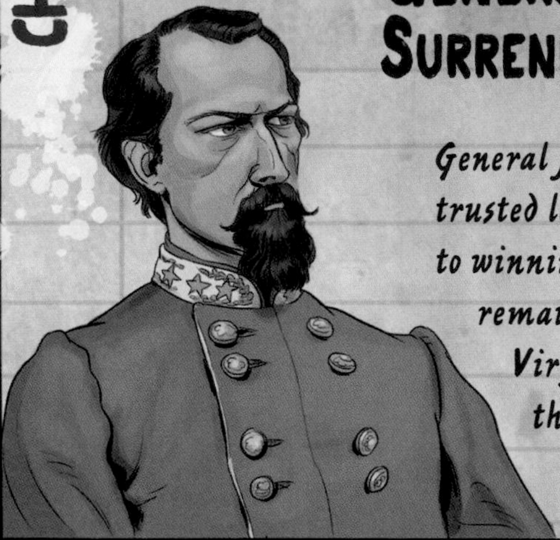

General John Brown Gordon was one of General Lee's most trusted leaders. By April 1865 Union forces were close to winning the war. They had surrounded Lee's small remaining army near Appomattox Court House, Virginia. Lee, Gordon, and their weary soldiers tried their best to fight one last good fight.

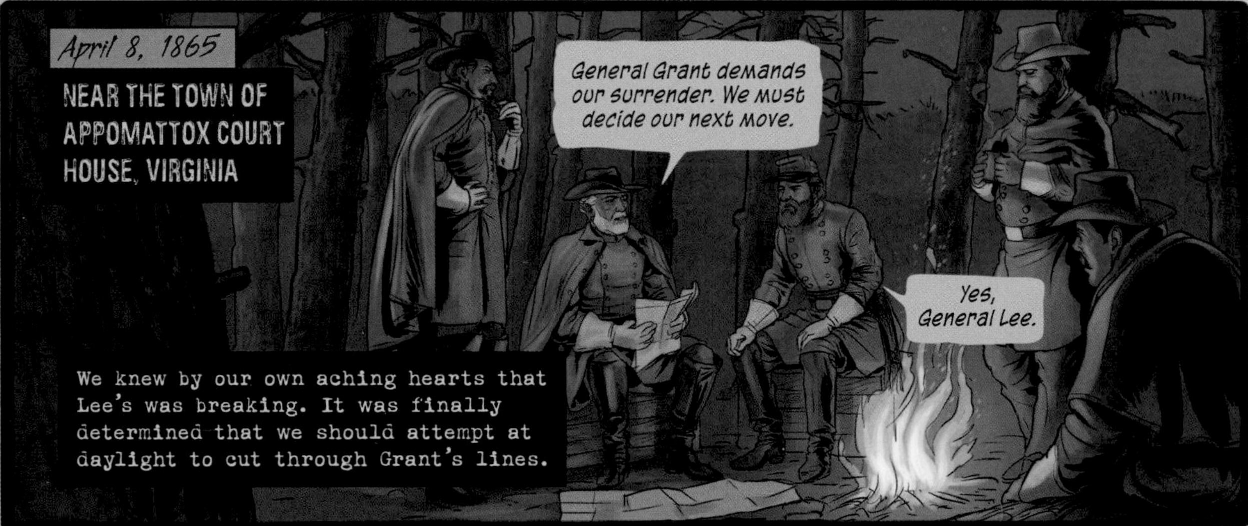

April 8, 1865
NEAR THE TOWN OF APPOMATTOX COURT HOUSE, VIRGINIA
General Grant demands our surrender. We must decide our next move.
Yes, General Lee.
We knew by our own aching hearts that Lee's was breaking. It was finally determined that we should attempt at daylight to cut through Grant's lines.

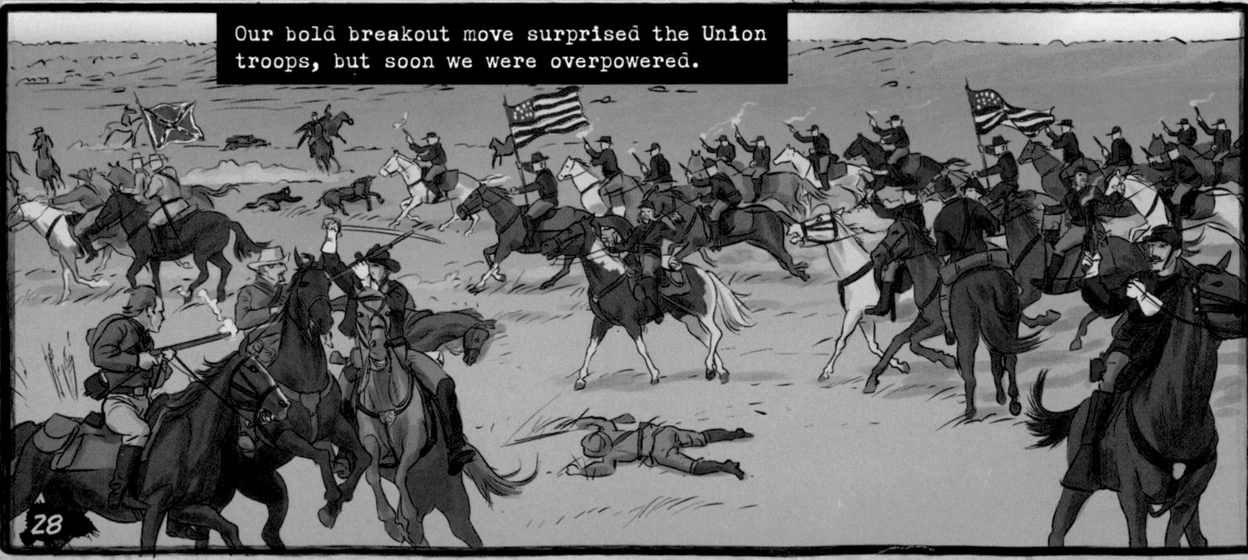

Our bold breakout move surprised the Union troops, but soon we were overpowered.

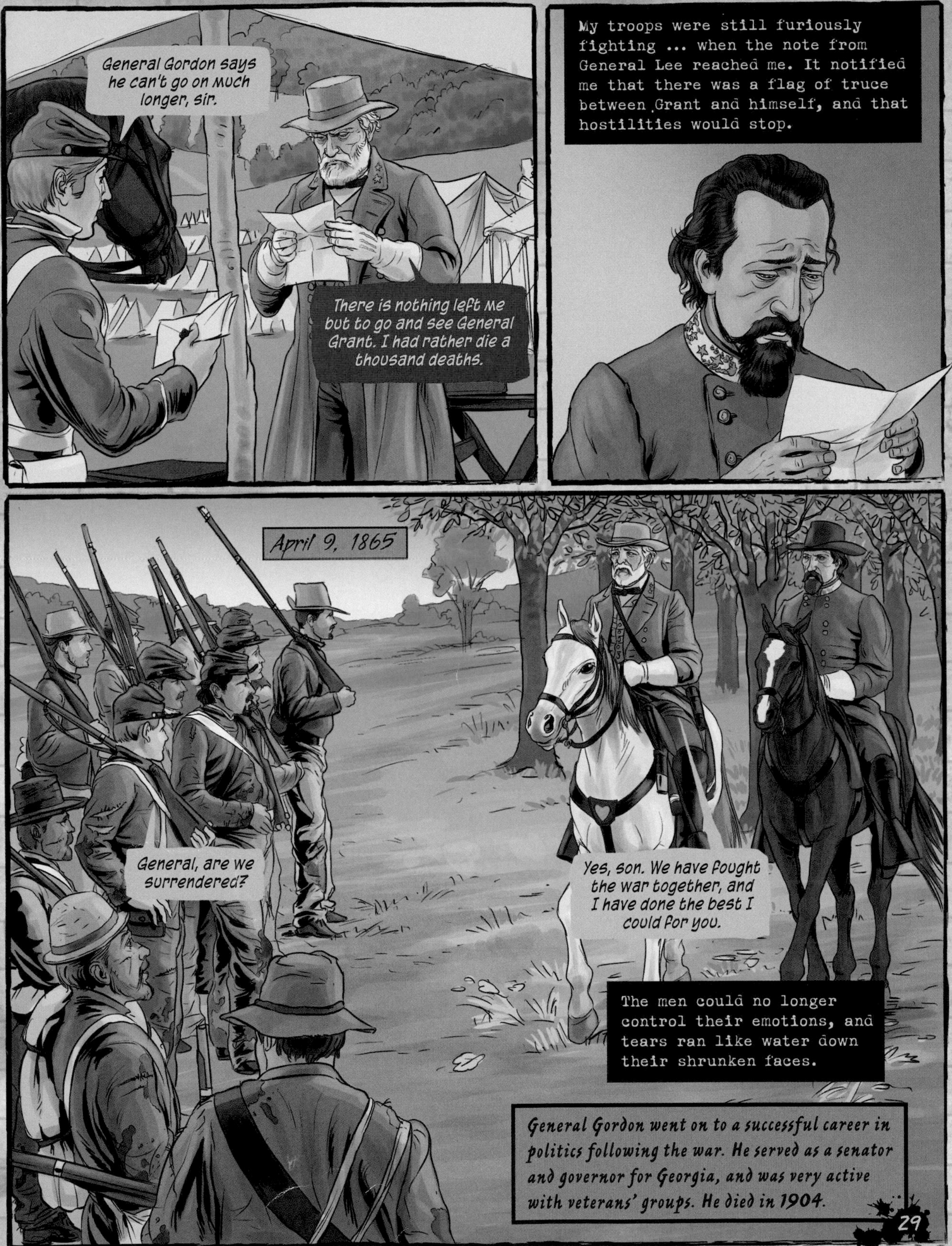
General Gordon says he can't go on much longer, sir.
There is nothing left me but to go and see General Grant. I had rather die a thousand deaths.
My troops were still furiously fighting ... when the note from General Lee reached me. It notified me that there was a flag of truce between Grant and himself, and that hostilities would stop.
April 9, 1865
General, are we surrendered?
Yes, son. We have fought the war together, and I have done the best I could for you.
The men could no longer control their emotions, and tears ran like water down their shrunken faces.
General Gordon went on to a successful career in politics following the war. He served as a senator and governor for Georgia, and was very active with veterans' groups. He died in 1904.

GLOSSARY

ARTILLERY (ar-TIL-uh-ree)—large, powerful guns that are usually mounted on wheels or tracks

BATTERY (BAT-uh-ree)—a group of heavy guns that are all used together

BROADSIDE (BRAHD-side)—a firing of all the guns on one side of a warship

CONFEDERACY (kuhn-FE-druh-see)—the Southern states that fought against the Northern states in the Civil War; also called the Confederate States of America

FEDERAL (FED-ur-uhl)—relating to the central government of the United States

GARRISON (GA-ruh-suhn)—a group of soldiers based in a town or in a fort

IRONCLAD (EYE-urn-klad)—a 19th-century warship with protective metal plates

REGIMENT (REJ-uh-muhnt)—a large group of soldiers who fight together as a unit

SECEDE (si-SEED)—to formally withdraw from a group or organization

SURRENDER (suh-REN-dur)—to give up or admit defeat

TRUCE (TROOSS)—a temporary agreement to stop fighting

TURRET (TUR-it)—a rotating structure on top of a military vehicle that holds a weapon

UNION (YOON-yuhn)—the United States of America

READ MORE

Garland, Sherry. *Voices of Gettysburg.* Gretna, La.: Pelican Pub. Co., 2010.

Marsico, Katie. *Great Battles of the Civil War.* Events in American History. Vero Beach, Fla.: Rourke Pub., 2010.

Nemeth, Jason D. *Voices of the Civil War: Stories from the Battlefields.* Voices of War. Mankato, Minn.: Capstone Press, 2011.

INTERNET SITES

FactHound offers a safe, fun way to find Internet sites related to this book. All sites on FactHound have been researched by our staff.
Here's all you do:

Visit www.facthound.com

Type in this code: 9781429686242

Super-cool stuff!

Check out projects, games and lots more at
www.capstonekids.com

INDEX

Anderson, Robert, 6, 8

Armistead, Lewis, 26

Battles
  Battle of Antietam,
    5, 20-23
  Battle of Appomattox
    Court House, 28-29
  Battle of
    Chancellorville, 5
  Battle of Gettysburg,
    5, 24-27
  Battle of Shiloh, 5
  Battle of the
    Wilderness, 5
  First Battle of Bull
    Run, 5, 10-13
  Fort Sumter, 4, 6-9
  Monitor vs. *Merrimac*,
    5, 14-19

Burnside, Ambrose, 20

Civil War
  cause of, 4
  dead, number of, 4
  end of, 4, 5, 29
  key dates of, 5
  start of, 4, 5

English, Samuel, 10-13

Gordon, John, 28-29

Grant, Ulysses S., 28

Greene, Samuel Dana,
    14-19

Lee, Robert E., 5, 24,
    27, 28, 29

Lee, Stephen, 6-9

Lincoln, Abraham, 4

Longstreet, James,
    24-27

Pickett, George, 24, 27

slavery, 4

Thompson, David, 20-23

U.S. Navy, 14-19

women soldiers, 27

Worden, John, 14,
    17, 18